STEP BY STEP
Fishing

Marshall Cavendish London & New York

Text prepared and edited by *Angling Times*
Written and collated by Peter Maskell.
'The Roach' is reproduced by kind permission of David Belcham.
Fish illustrations by Keith Linsell.

Published by Marshall Cavendish Books Limited,
58 Old Compton Street,
London W1V 5PA

Reproduction and film make up by
The Pentagon Printing Group, Soho Square, London W1V 5TW

First printed 1977

ISBN 0 85685 319 4

Printed and bound in Great Britain by
R. J. Acford Ltd., Industrial Estate, Chichester, Sussex

Contents

Coarse Fishing

Basic tackle 6
How to cast 9
Freshwater baits 14
Floats 20
Legering 30
Two basic knots 36
Roach 38
Bream 40
Chub 42
Perch 44
Pike 46

Sea Fishing

Basic tackle 50
How to cast 53
Sea baits 58
Beach fishing 63
Boat fishing 67
Pier fishing 71
Sea floats 76
Cod 78
Bass 80
Plaice 82
Tope 84
Mullet 86
Index 88

Coarse fishing

Coarse fishing is by far the largest branch of angling. There are an estimated two million coarse fishermen in the United Kingdom and the number grows each year. The heaviest concentrations of anglers are to be found in the industrial conurbations of England.

To the city dweller, angling offers the ideal hobby, providing both sport and relaxation. Coarse fishing can be as cheap or as expensive as the angler cares to make it. Tackle costs and travelling can be kept to a minimum and outlay on bait need not be great.

A variety of fishing, ranging from rivers and canals to pits, ponds and lakes is available to the angler. The quality varies enormously from the hard-fished canals of the North, where the angler can expect no more than a few pounds of small fish, to the fertile slow-moving drains and rivers of Eastern England.

Most coarse fishermen belong to a local angling club. Angling is a gregarious sport and rising rates, rents and inflation have forced anglers to band together to protect their fishing.

It is the club structure of coarse fishing that has bred a highly professional competitive spirit among anglers. Every weekend during the season thousands of matchmen take part in club and open matches. They have developed the most successful fish catching techniques and passed them on to fellow anglers.

Basic tackle

The newcomer to coarse fishing is often bewildered by the wide range of tackle decorating the walls of his local dealer. The dozens of different types of rod and reel on display will range in price from a few pounds to well over £30.

The wrong choice can leave you out of pocket and with the wrong type of tackle for the waters you hope to fish. In this chapter the beginner will find a guide to the best tackle to buy which, carefully chosen, should last a lifetime.

Rods

Rods are the most important item of angling equipment. A good rod will last for years and it is vital that you choose one which is long enough, light enough and with the correct action. Split cane and Spanish reed rods are a thing of the past. Lightweight tubular fibreglass is the material to choose and there is a tremendous range from which to select.

For float rods choose a 12–13 foot rod. Remember you will need a long rod, at least 10 feet in length, to give you casting accuracy, distance and control when playing a fish. Make sure all the rings on the rod are stand off rings and that it has a reasonably long handle with sliding reel fittings.

Test that the rod has been correctly ringed by attaching a reel and threading a line through the rings. Pull the end of the line so that the rod arches. If it is correctly ringed the line will follow the curve of the rod through the rings. If it is incorrectly ringed the line will cut from ring to ring at a sharp angle, especially on the top joint. Remember too that you may be holding the rod for hours on end—so make sure that it is not too heavy.

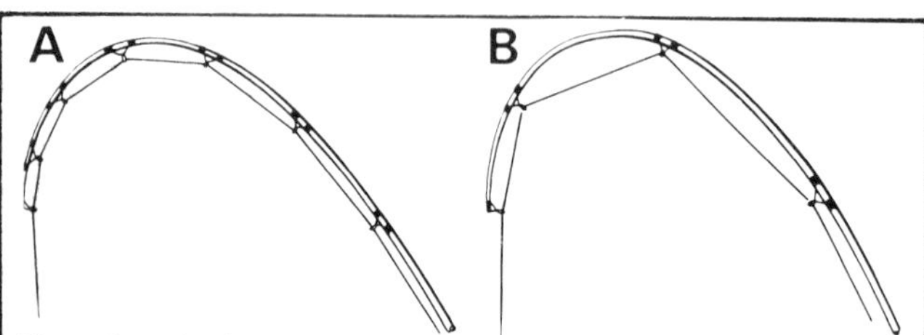

Drawing A shows a correctly ringed rod. Note how the line follows the curve of the rod. Drawing B shows a badly ringed rod with the line cutting from ring to ring at sharp angles.

Tip action rods are designed to speed up the strike and pick up line quickly. They are ideal for normal range float fishing for the major species. Rods with an all-through action are better suited to the specimen hunter—the angler after big barbel, tench and chub.

When buying a rod always consult a reputable tackle dealer or take an experienced angler with you. Remember that advice costs nothing and there is no substitute for experience when buying a rod. A separate rod will be needed for legering, but this type will be dealt with in a later chapter.

The angler lets the rod do the work as he draws a hooked fish towards the bank.

Reels

There are two types of reel commonly used in coarse fishing—the centre pin and the fixed spool reel. The centre pin looks the simpler of the two but far greater skill is required to master it. Buy a fixed spool reel first as they are easy to use and make casting an effortless exercise.

There are many makes on the market their prices ranging from a few pounds to £20. Like rods, a good reel, if properly maintained, will last for years and buying a cheap one could prove a false economy.

For proper casting it is essential to fill the reel spool correctly. Some manufacturers make reels with spools far too deep—spools that would take several hundred yards of line to fill. If the spool holds more than 100 yards of 5lb line then fill it up with old line or cotton before winding on the line you will use for fishing. When correctly filled the line should reach within a $\frac{1}{8}$ inch of the spool lip, ensuring that the line peels off easily—an essential aid to correct casting.

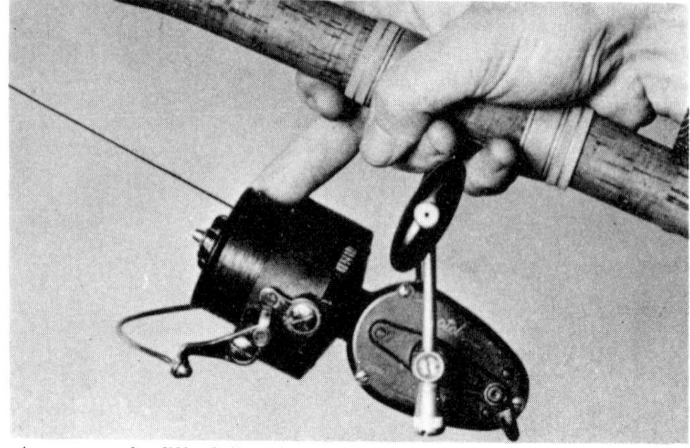

A correctly filled fixed spool reel.

Lines

Buy a nylon monofilament line best suited to your rod. Most float rods work best with lines of between two and four pounds breaking strain. Avoid fine lines if you are a beginner, and choose a line of $2\frac{1}{2}$–3lb. It will be adequate for most species of fish. Do not forget that even modern lines can lose much of their strength and elasticity quite quickly. Check your line regularly and if it shows signs of deterioration buy a new one.

Floats

There are dozens of floats on the market and a lot of them are designed to catch anglers not fish! Many of them are designed for specific types of fishing and are useless for other types. Some of the main types are dealt with in later chapters. Buy a selection after consulting an experienced angler or a reputable tackle dealer. They have the experience to make sure your floats are best suited to the water you will fish.

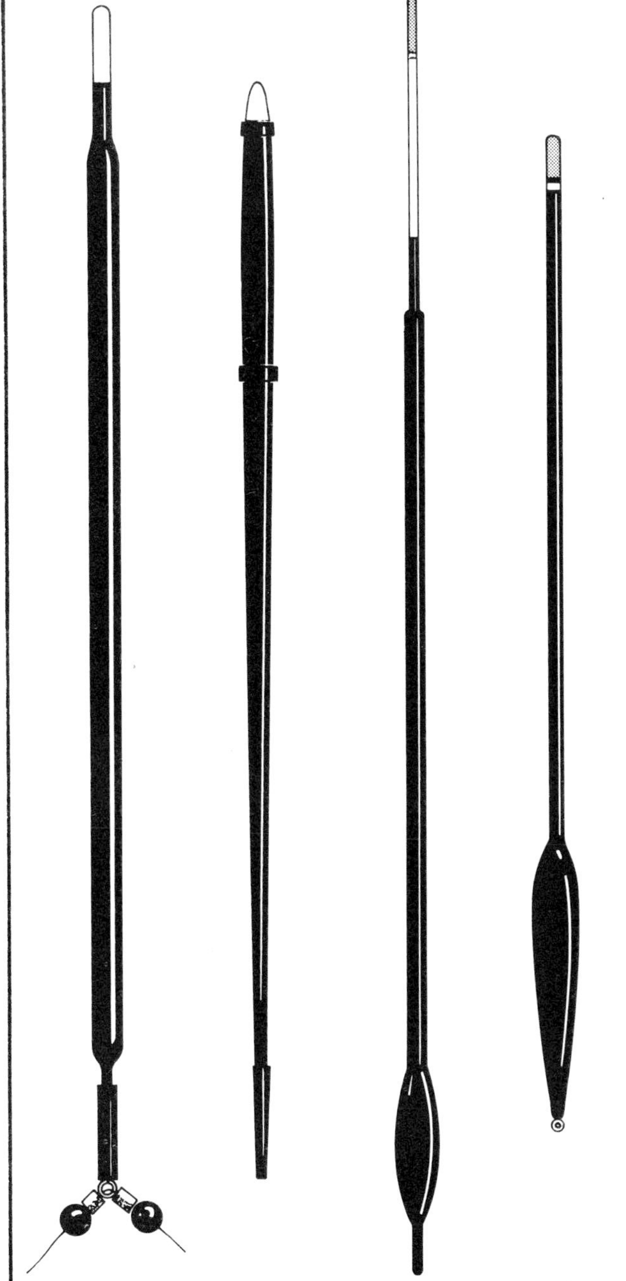

Examples of some of the many kinds of floats. From left to right, waggler, stick and two types of antenna.

Shots and weights

Shots are merely small lead balls split along one side. They aid casting, balance the float and present the bait to the fish in a natural manner. The largest used by anglers is the swan shot. The next largest is the AAA: BB and Numbers 1 to 10. Buy a selection of shot, the softer the better, and keep them in grit free containers.

A selection of split shot in grit free containers. Always buy the softest shot possible.

Nets

You will need two nets: a keepnet to retain your catch until the end of the day, and a landing net to lift large specimens. Buy the largest keepnet you can afford and choose one with a knotless mesh. This will help prevent damage to your catch.

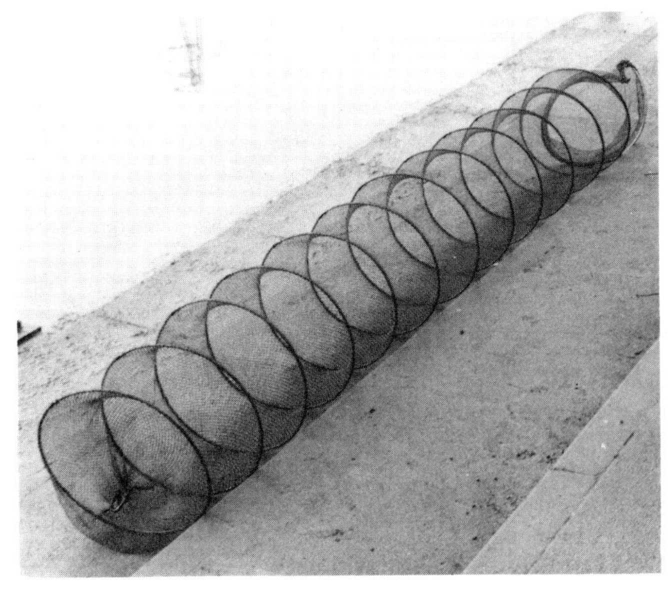

A knotless keepnet will help prevent damage to the angler's catch. It is best to buy the largest net you can afford.

Hooks

Like floats, hooks come in a variety of types and sizes. Eyed hooks are ideal for some kinds of fishing but not for general coarse fishing. Choose spade-end hooks

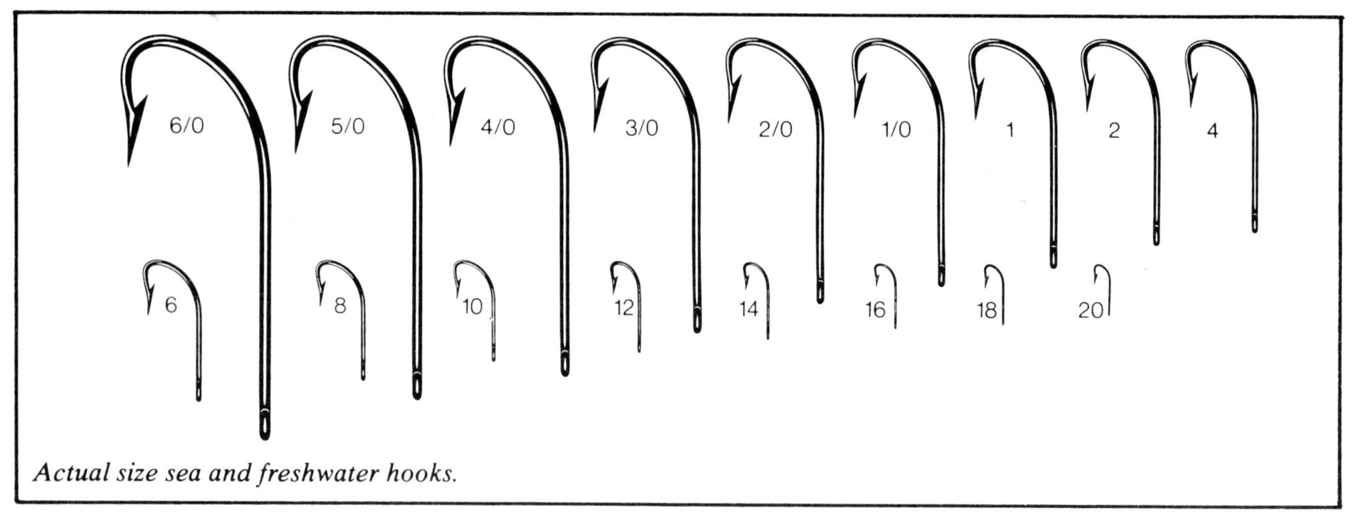

Actual size sea and freshwater hooks.

ranging from size 10, suitable for big baits like bread, down to the smaller size 18, more suited to small, fragile baits like maggot.

Baskets

To keep your tackle neat and tidy you will need a basket or tackle carrier. Whichever you choose make sure it is large so that you can pack all your tackle in it. It can also be used as a seat.

A fishing basket

Umbrella

Anglers' umbrellas are as vital to the comfort of the angler as a good set of waterproofs. They provide shelter from the rain and from cold winds. Buy a large one and you will be able to keep not only yourself but also all your tackle dry.

The small forked rod rests are best suited to supporting the butt of the rod, not the tip.

Other accessories

Disgorgers are used to unhook deeply hooked fish. Buy either the barrel or button type. Never use the simple V-shaped disgorger which is crude and can damage the fish.

You will also need rod rests, bait tins, a bowl for mixing groundbait, and a rod holdall to protect your rods, bank sticks and a landing net handle.

How to cast

Accurate casting is one of the many keys to success in angling. Yet this basic skill is often neglected by both the beginner and the experienced angler. Fish are essentially shoal fish, picking their feeding places according to the natural contours of the river bed. With careful groundbaiting, and a knowledge of his swim the angler can usually encourage the fish to feed in a position that suits him—that is a position within easy casting distance. Having done this he must be certain he can cast to the same spot time and time again.

Casting should be effortless. If the tackle is properly balanced and correctly weighted the rod will do all the work. There will be no need for the angler to use physical power to cast his float to the required spot.

The overhead cast

The overhead cast is the cast you will use for long range fishing with a float on such waters as the Welland, Witham, Huntspill, Warwickshire Avon.

Basic requirements to get the best out of the cast are: a 13 foot rod, open faced fixed spool reel, and a full spool of line in the 1½lb to 2½lb range—the actual choice depending on the size of float and the amount of shot is carries.

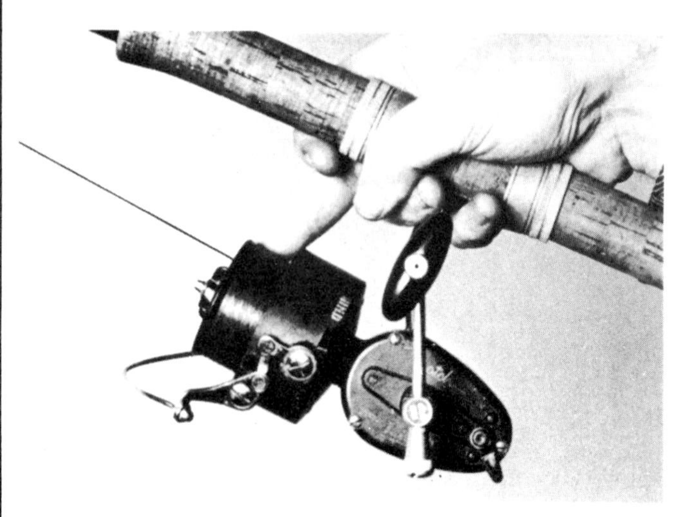

1. *The position of the finger, locking the line to the rim of the spool.*

3. *The rod is now at the maximum of the back cast—that is roughly the 2 o'clock position. The move forward into the cast is about to begin.*

2. *The rod begins its travel backward behind the caster. Note the cast is two handed. The reel is placed high up on the butt so there is maximum effective distance between the two hands. This aids accuracy.*

4. *The rod begins to arch as it travels forward with the cast. The rod shows the pressure taking effect, which is creating the spring that will project the float across the river. Both hands are rigid.*

5. *The float is away. It goes zooming out across the river. The finger has been lifted off the lip of the spool and the angler is 'feathering' line from the spool to ensure the float reaches the required position. Note that the rod tip has lost its compression and is flexing backwards as a reaction against the loss of pressure.*

6. *The follow through is underway. The rod continues its forward movement. In the previous picture the right arm was slightly bent. Now notice the right arm is rigid and locking the rod in the fixed position.*

7. *The finished cast. The rod has completed its movement from 2 o'clock to 8.30—in an anti-clockwise sequence. Now begin the process of gathering up any slack line.*

8. *The back view (taken just prior to picture 6 in this sequence). It shows the right arm rigid and thus playing the part of an extension of the rod during the cast.*

9. *This shows what the caster is out to achieve. Note the two splashes occurring simultaneously as the float and shot hit the water almost together. This allows the bait to sink properly.*

The swingtip cast

The object of swingtip casting must be accuracy with a limited expenditure of effort. This is because the bomb must not thump the surface as it lands.

If this illustrated cast is used, the swingtip itself is able to go through its circular movement without the line tangling around the end ring.

Accuracy is achieved when the rod points directly into the sky in the vertical position throughout the cast. This means the bomb cannot wander upstream or downstream.

1. *The back view. The rod is held completely vertically. The lead and rod tip are beginning their move as the impetus for the cast gets underway.*

2. *The side view as the bomb reaches its maximum backward position. The rod comes under the first part of compression as the angler begins the forward movement by extending the bent right arm and pulling with the left.*

3. *The follow-through is under way. The moment of maximum compression of the rod has passed and the lead is already projecting outwards. The tension has gone from the swingtip and it is moving from a rear to forward position.*

4. *The rod is now almost straight. The swingtip is folding over to face the direction of the cast. The rod is pointing directly at the spot where the bomb is required to hit the surface of the river.*

The position of the rod during the cast decides this accuracy factor, while the elevation of the bomb allied to the power employed during flight decides whether or not you reach or overshoot the target area, but power itself is kept to an absolute minimum to prevent that so-important lack of surface impact.

Ideally, make sure you use enough power to exceed the spot you want to reach and then, by feathering the line as it leaves the spool (with the index finger of the right hand) brake the flight of the bomb so that it falls on the desired spot.

Recommended line breaking strain is 2lb to 3lb.

5. *The bomb's flight continues across the water. The rod has followed through to the 9 o'clock position.*

6. *The back view of a good cast. The rod has remained in the vertical position throughout, which ensures the bomb flights accurately.*

7. *How not to do it. The rod is in the 2 o'clock position from which it is virtually impossible to cast accurately.*

Freshwater baits

The major species of coarse fish can be caught on a great variety of baits. Large and small specimens have been taken on orange peel, bananas, silver paper and cornflakes. The list of baits is endless, so this chapter is restricted to those most widely used and shows you how to prepare them.

Maggots

The most popular coarse fishing bait is the maggot. It is readily available from tackle shops, easy to use and will take most species of fish. Maggots are the larvae of different kinds of flies, including the bluebottle, greenbottle and the ordinary housefly. They are usually sold by the pint.

Maggots must be kept clean and in a container with a plentiful supply of air. In hot weather they quickly turn into chrysalises, so it is important to keep them cool. After buying your maggots, riddle out the sawdust in which they have been placed and remove any dead skins in the batch. Place them in a clean, well-ventilated bait tin, a quarter full of slightly dampened bran. The bran will keep the maggots cool and clean as they wriggle through it.

Never fill a bait container more than half full with maggots and bran. Put more in and the quality of the bait will suffer. Always buy your maggots at least two days before your fishing trip. This will allow you to prepare them properly.

Maggots can be bought in various colours. Under certain conditions yellow, bronze or pink maggots will catch fish when the ordinary white maggot will fail. Alternatively you can colour them yourself by buying a powder maggot dye. Chrysodine powder will produce a yellowy-orange maggot. Simply pour boiling water into some of the powder, let it cool and then add a few drops to your maggots. Put them into clean fine sawdust and they will absorb the colour.

There are several other kinds of maggots which are also useful both for hookbait and groundbait. The most widely used are the pinkie and the squat. Both types are much smaller than the ordinary maggot.

The pinkie has a very faint pink tinge, and is an extremely active maggot. It is also a very hardy one.

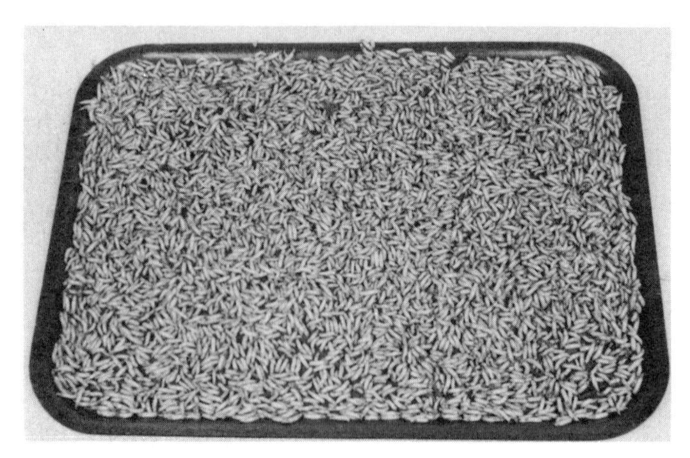

A tray of maggots, the most popular coarse fishing bait. They are readily available from tackle shops.

A caster is a maggot chrysalis that must be used during the early stages of its development so that it will sink.

Wheat is prepared in the same way as hemp. Simmer the grains until they swell and the kernels split.

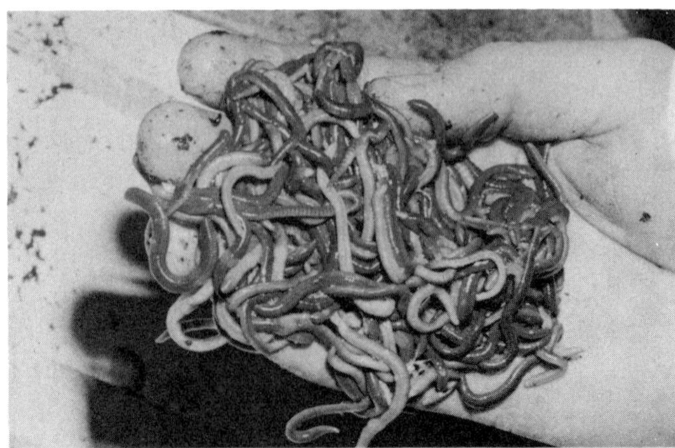

The natural movement of worms makes them effective bait for chub, perch, bream, roach and tench.

Always keep this kind dry and in a sealed container. Pinkies are used mainly with groundbait to attract fish into the swim. However, fished on a small hook, they make a deadly hookbait.
Squats are slightly smaller than the pinkie but white and far less active. They are used in groundbait as an attracter for bream shoals. In arduous conditions they often make a tempting hookbait.
Gozzers are often used by matchmen on bream waters. Soft and white, they are simply home-bred maggots which have been fed on poultry.

When using maggots as hookbait it is important to hook them properly. Nick the maggot gently through the flap of skin at the blunt end, taking care not to burst it.

Casters

During the last ten years the caster has become one of the most widely used baits in coarse fishing. A bait for roach, bream, chub and dace, it is simply a maggot chrysalis. When a maggot first changes to a caster it remains white, turning gradually to a red-brown and then dark red. It is only during the early stages of this development that it will sink and is then of most use to the angler.

Freshness is even more vital than with the maggot. Like maggots they can be bought by the pint from tackle shops, sealed in air-tight polythene bags. Keep them as cool as possible—if you have access to a fridge, so much the better. Properly bagged and kept in a refrigerator they will last for several days, but always try to buy them as near your fishing trip as possible. When you get to the bankside remove them from the bag, place them in a clean bait tin and moisten with water. This helps arrest their natural development and stops them turning to floaters during your day's session. Do not be tempted to keep your casters in water too long. After a day or so they will quickly sour.

You can prepare your own casters by buying several pints of maggots and riddling off the casters twice a day as they turn naturally. After each riddle place the casters in plastic bags and pop them in the fridge.

When baiting with single casters, insert the hook, which should be no larger than a size 16, in one of the two eyes at the blunt end of the bait. Tap the hook point down and round and bury the hook shank in the

A killing bait for roach, hemp and tares are strictly limited to the summer and autumn months.

When using maggots as hookbait, nick the hook gently through the flap of skin at the blunt end of the maggot.

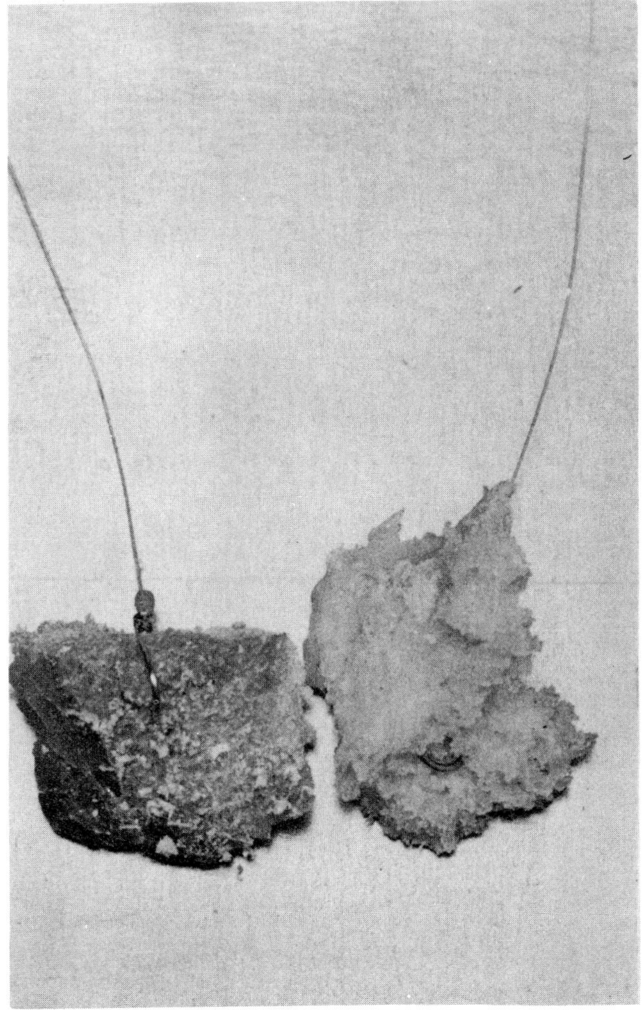

Bread is one of the simplest baits to use. It can be used as flake or as crust or paste.

bait. Double or treble casters are hooked in the same way as maggots.

Bread

One of the simplest baits of all, bread can be used as flake simply by pulling lumps of the fluffy middle from the loaf, or as crust or paste.

To make paste take a clean cloth and place a handful of white crumb from a stale loaf into it. Run it under the cold tap and knead the bread into a paste. Always ensure this bait is on the soft side. Hard paste may stay on the hook longer—but it will not catch many fish. Bread baits are often more effective in the summer months, although they can be used in winter floods.

Seed baits

These are strictly limited to the summer and autumn months. But they give the beginner his best chance of taking a memorable bag of roach. On many waters roach will feed madly on seed baits under conditions where other baits will hardly yield a bite.

The two best baits are hemp and tares. Both are easily obtainable from tackle shops or pet shops and are cheap to use. Half a pint of hemp and a teacupful of tares is sufficient for a day's fishing.

Hemp Prepare hemp by putting it into a saucepan of water, bring it to the boil and simmer until the white shoots peep out. There is no need to pass the hook through the seed-simply press the hook bend into the split.

Tares Soak tares overnight in cold water and then bring them to the boil in a saucepan. Simmer gently until they turn rubbery; take care not to split the tough outer skin. Just nick the hook through the skin, do not try to pass it completely through the seed.

Tares are much larger than grains of hemp—and very filling too. When fishing them together throw in no more than a dozen grains of hemp each cast and use tares on the hook.

Wheat This bait is prepared in the same way as hemp. Simmer the grains until they swell and the kernels split, revealing the white inside.

Worms

Natural baits that are easy to gather, worms will take most species of fish. The movement of the worm makes it an effective bait for chub, perch, bream, roach and tench, especially when the water is coloured or freezing.

The largest worm is the lobworm and is best fished on a large hook for big fish. Redworms and brandlings are found together in manure heaps and make superb winter baits. Usuaully they are about four inches long and can be fished either singly or in bunches.

Cheese and luncheon meat

These two baits are predominantly chub and barbel baits, although cheese makes an excellent summer bait for roach. Luncheon meat can be cut into ready to use cubes or kneaded into a paste.

Preparing hemp and ta

1. *The tares (left) and the hemp are ready for cooking.*

4. *Here the tares are brought to the boil.*

7. *The finished tares.*

2. *Add bicarbonate of soda.*

3. *Then soak them in water.*

5. *The tares are now soft and ready for the hook. Drain off the hot water.*

6. *Add some sugar to give them a gleam.*

8. *A bait for a big roach . . . a tare on a hook.*

9. *Hemp—a top summer tempter for roach.*

Preparing casters

1. *A half gallon of maggots is passed through a riddle. This removes dead and dying maggots and gets the maggots into fresh sawdust.*

2. *Moisten the sawdust. Not too much water . . . but enough to leave it permanently damp. If you soak them they will climb out.*

3. *Casters begin to turn. You see the first signs as the casters are pushed up by the live maggots underneath. White casters will quickly colour when contained in polythene bags and at the waterside.*

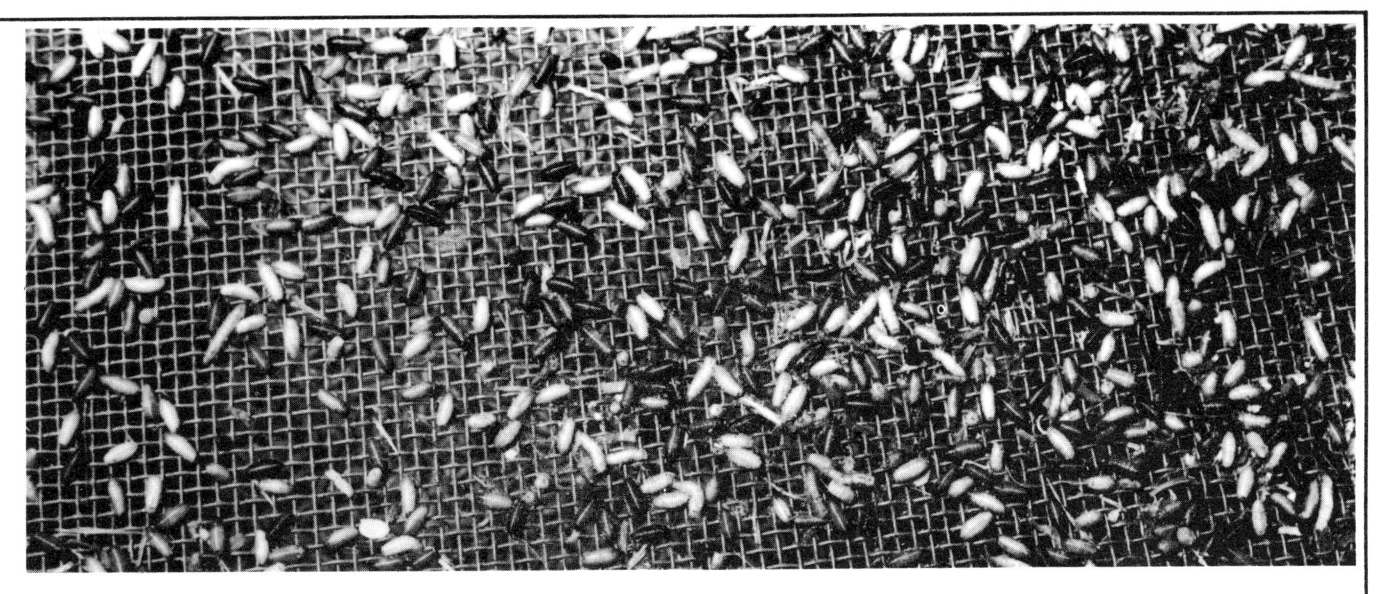

4. *Riddle again and collect your casters. This process is repeated twice a day until you have all you need.*

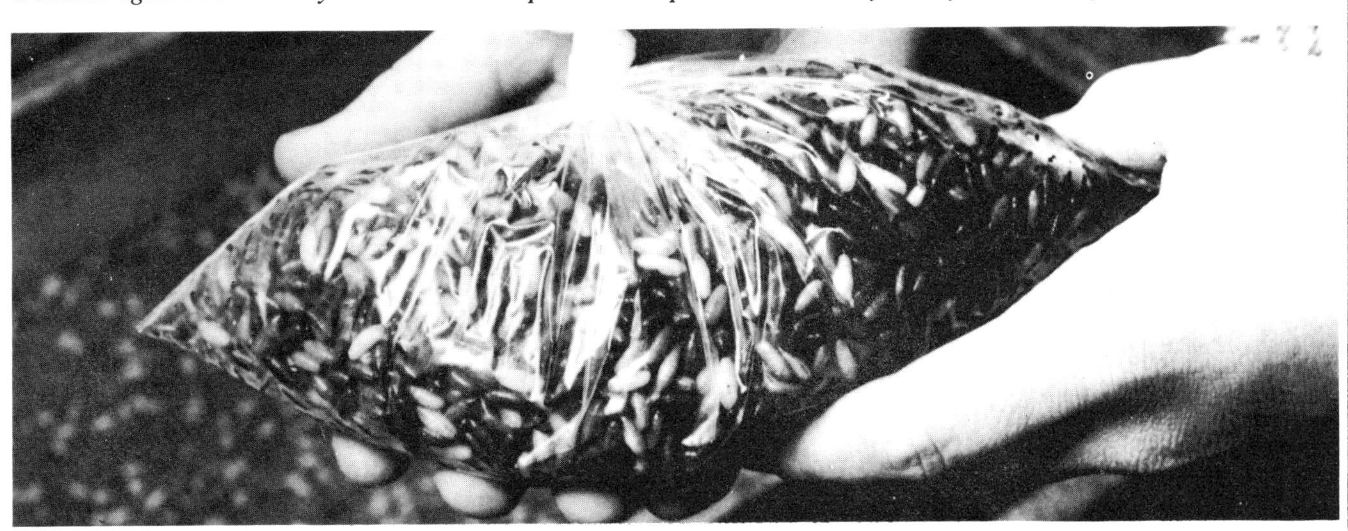

5. *Each batch is placed in a polythene bag, knotted or sealed tightly to ensure they do not become floaters.*

6. *The finished product—top quality casters that are the best obtainable.*

Floats

Floats fascinate! Nearly every angler will have a box full of different coloured, sized and shaped floats which he has acquired over the seasons. Each year new types are brought onto the market and only the strong willed can resist the brightly coloured display cards in the local tackle shop.

The beginner will be faced by a huge selection of floats. Always ask expert advice whenever possible and select those types most suited to the waters you will be fishing.

Quill floats—one of the few kinds of floats on the market twenty years ago—are still a useful addition to your float box. Make sure you have a selection of porcupine and peacock quills, as they can be used on virtually every kind of water.

For fast flowing waters the beginner will need a selection of stick and balsa floats. For still or sluggish waters he should choose the antenna type. In the following pages five major types of float, and how to use them, are described in detail. Master the separate techniques and you will be well on your way to becoming a skilled float fisherman.

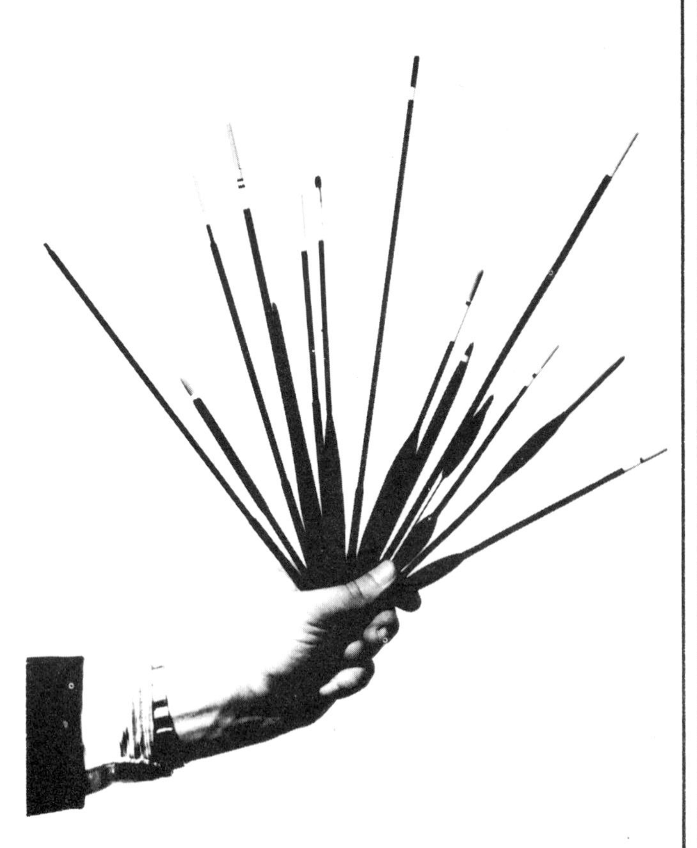

A handful of floats that will deal with most water conditions the angler is likely to encounter. The floats range from antennas and zoomers for still and slow moving waters to sticks and Avons for flowing water.

The waggler

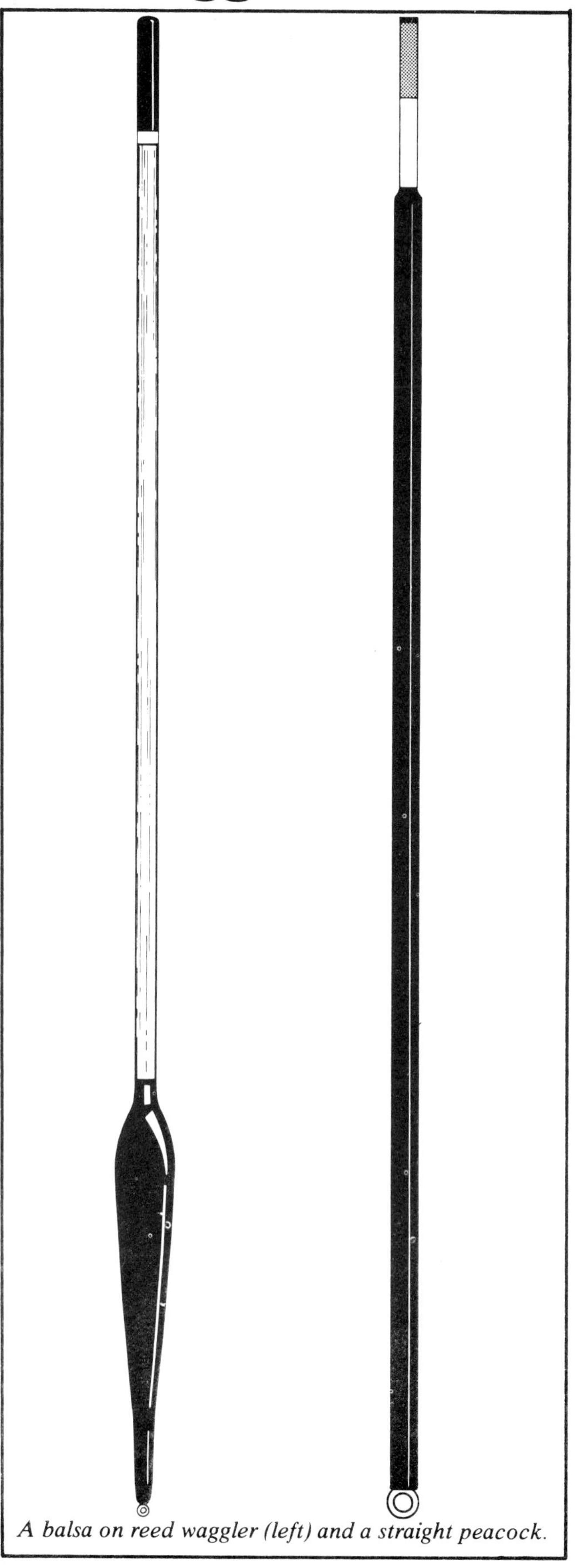

A balsa on reed waggler (left) and a straight peacock.

It is not always possible to catch fish close-in on running water. In summer months you may need to fish well out. Then the normal stick float becomes difficult to control, particularly if the wind is downstream. To overcome these conditions on wide fast-flowing rivers like the Trent and Severn, match fishermen came up with the waggler.

Basically an antenna float with, or without, a slender body, the waggler has proved highly successful. It is not so much a particular float . . . more a particular method for which many antenna floats can be made to work.

Buoyancy

A waggler must have a buoyant tip to withstand the pull of the current. So a medium-sized peacock quill antenna is an ideal choice. Fished bottom end only to beat any wind, the float stands up in the current and waggles on the retrieve. Hence its nickname.

The waggler is used when you need to cast well out into midstream. At least an inch of float should be left standing out of the water. This will allow you to check the float when mending line without it disappearing below the surface. It is also less likely to sink if the bottom shot drags too much on the bed.

With the waggler, the float travels downstream *ahead* of the bait—the complete opposite of the stick float where the bait travels downstream ahead of the float. A fish facing upstream intercepting the bait will cause the float to disappear.

Line control is obviously more difficult with the waggler. If there is a downstream wind, you must sink the line. Otherwise keep the rod high and any belly in the line to a minimum.

After a time, you will learn to recognise a predictable up-and-down rhythm as the waggler rides through the swim. If it rises out of the water, or stays down longer than normal it could be fish.

Wagglers first made their impact on the Severn and Warwickshire Avon where anglers needed to catch chub well out in midstream. With a bold biting fish like the chub, there was no need for the float to be shotted down. The waggler just vanished as the chub made off with the bait, usually casters.

Shotting

One of the beauties of the waggler is how it shows bites on the drop. For far-bank chub fishing—now common practice on southern rivers like the Thames and Lee—the shot are grouped round the float locking it to the line. This gives the weight for casting. A light shot is all that is needed on the line, allowing the bait to fall in a natural arc.

Heavy loose-feeding with casters brings the chub up off the bottom. Away goes the float, as you take chub on the drop.

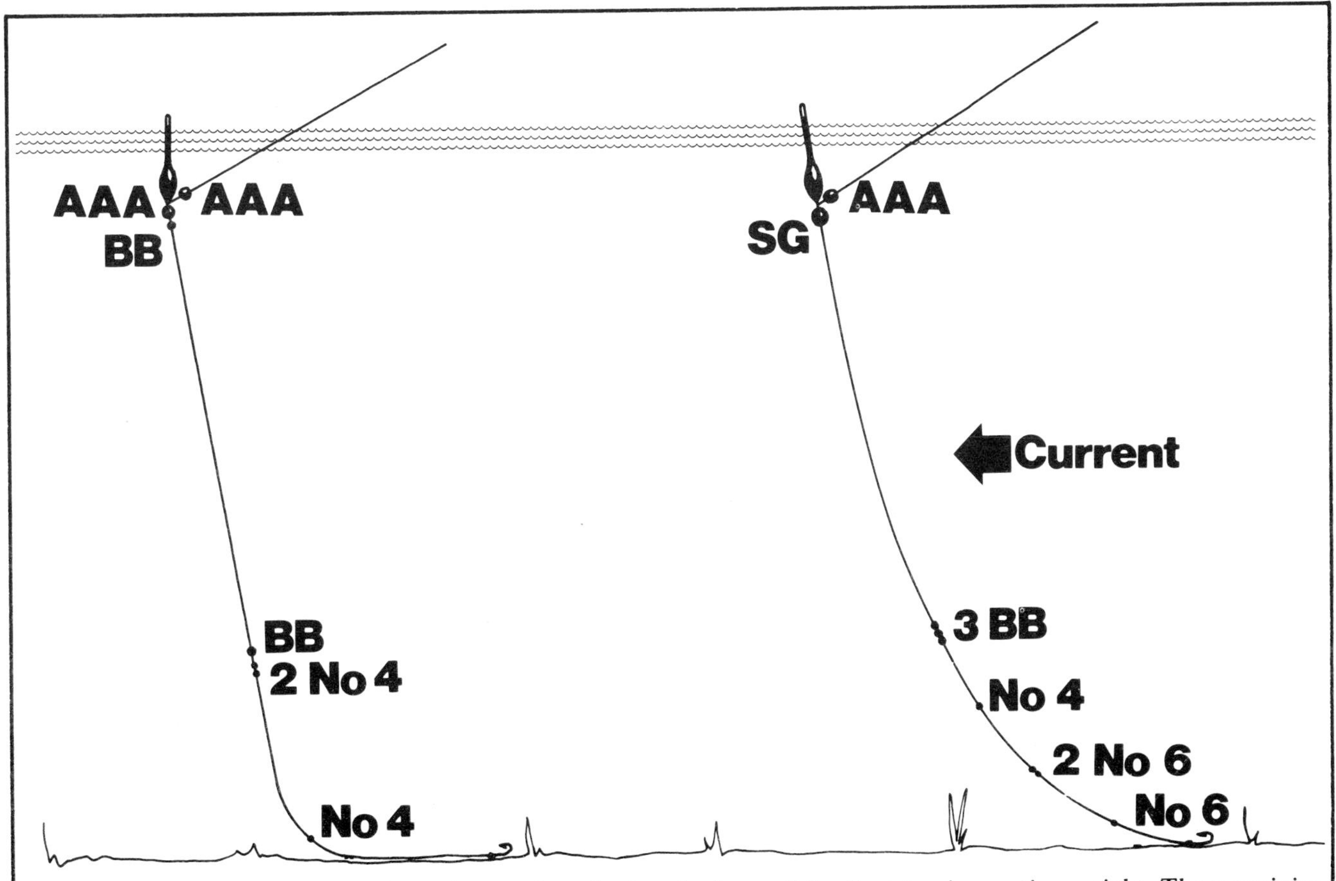

How to shot the waggler. Note how shot are bunched at the base of the float to give casting weight. The remaining shot are grouped down the line to give delicate bait presentation

The antenna

There are more variations on the antenna float than any other model. The angler is confronted with duckers, missiles, zoomers, darts, wagglers and swingers. It is important to understand that they are all variations of the same basic antenna float designed to do different jobs. By using various materials in the float's manufacture, each has varying qualities.

Basically the antenna float is designed for fishing still or very slow-moving water where there is some depth. So it is used on all lakes and wide rivers where long casting is necessary.

The first designs

The first antenna floats were simple bird quills with a cork body at the base. The cork gave the float buoyancy; the quill sensitivity. With the float fished bottom-end only it proved an ideal combination, especially for shy roach in still water.

The next step was a larger antenna float designed to carry more shot and cast further. Elder pith took over from cork because it was easier to shape, and carried more shot. Cane took over from bird quill because it was less buoyant and sank easier with a bite.

By painting the straight cane stem with different coloured bands, lift and drop bites could easily be detected. So the first bream float was born. Balsa has now replaced elder pith and cork for float bodies, but cane is still used for the most sensitive antenna tips. Modest bites are magnified by the slim antenna, but the float becomes difficult to see at long range.

As much bream fishing is carried out at distance it became necessary to look for a new material that would take plenty of shot, yet be sensitive enough to show shy bream bites. Peacock quill was the answer as it was very buoyant and could carry plenty of shot for casting. It was found naturally and in long straight lengths so proved ideal for making into ultra-long floats which could beat any surface drift.

With the line sunk below the surface from rod tip to float, the angler could fish his ground-baited patch regardless of wind. And the thickest tip of the peacock float could be seen at a distance. A small balsa body added stability.

When supplies of peacock quill became scarce three years ago, float makers looked around for a new material and came up with sarkandas or Indian reed. It has similar qualities to peacock, with the added advantage of being straighter, but it is more difficult to paint.

Modern techniques

To add more sensitivity to antenna floats, matchmen have added cane inserts to the tips. These show lift and drop bites more clearly with the float lifting up in the water.

The modern trend is to lock the antenna float to the line with shot either side of the bottom eye. This gives

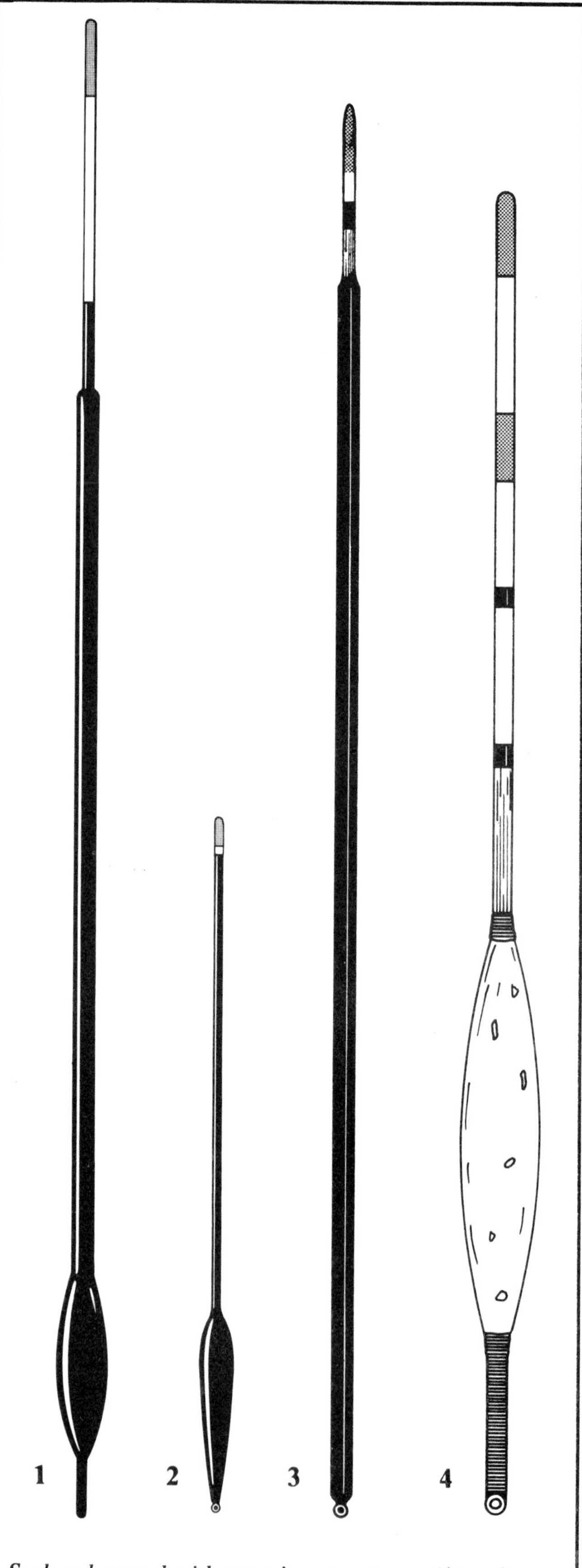

Sarkandas reed with cane insert antenna (1) and cane with balsa body antenna (2).
Drinking straw with cane insert straight antenna (3) and original elder pith on cane antenna float (4).

weight for casting as well as maintaining depth. Some matchmen go further than this, fitting a tiny swivel to the bottom of the float so that it collapses on the strike and the float can be changed without having to break the line.

As a general rule the shot are always bulked on the line just below halfway between float and bait. This is done to prevent tangles on the cast. A small shot on the hooklength can act as a tell-tale. If the fish lifts it off the bottom, the float simply rises in the water—the classic lift bite.

On the other days when fish are feeding off the bottom, use the antenna to look for bites on the drop. If the thin antenna stays out of the water by the time it should have settled, a fish must have taken the bait and be holding up the shot. This is the moment to strike.

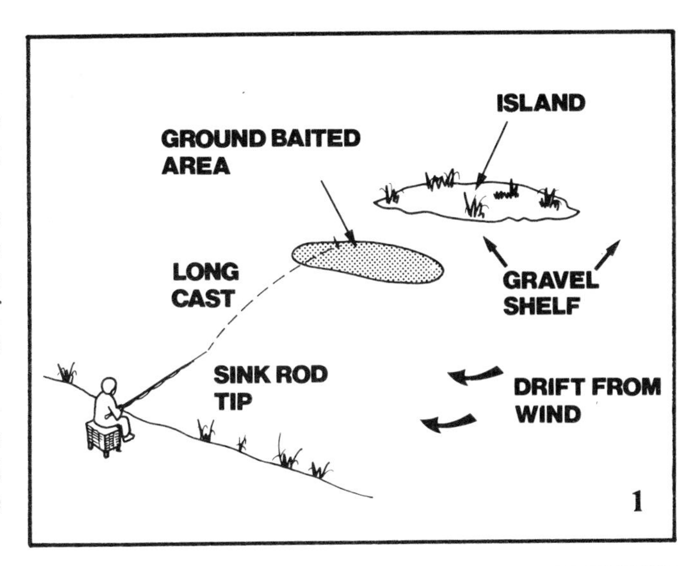

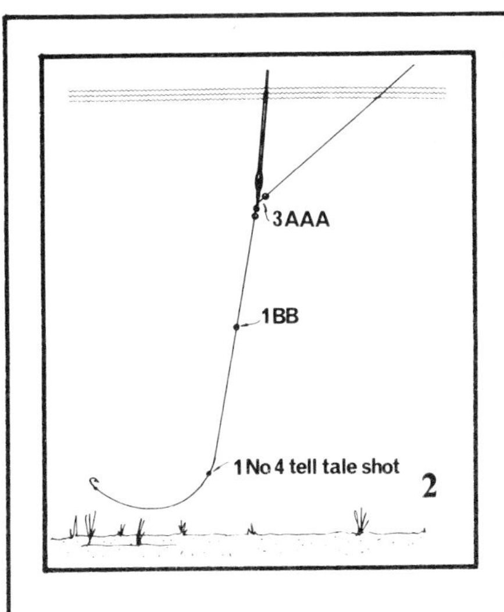

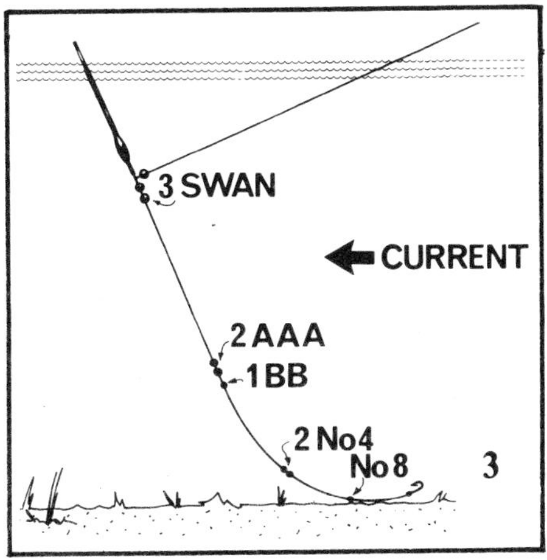

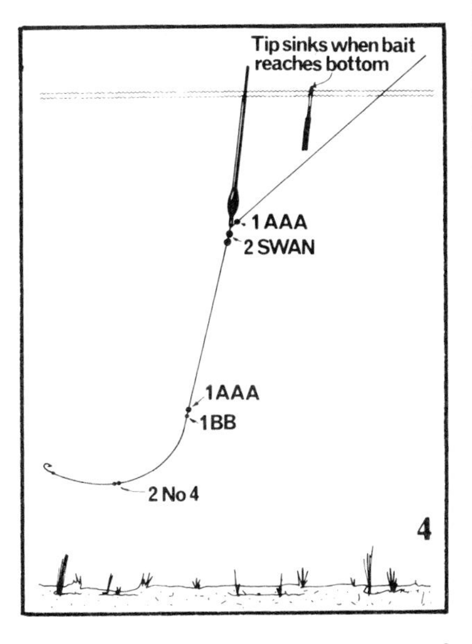

1. *An ideal swim for using the antenna.*

2. *This is a 3½ AAA reed antenna with cane insert shotted up for drop bite fishing. The main shot is locked round the float to give casting weight.*

3. *A 4½ swan peacock antenna shotted up as a waggler. The float moves slowly downstream ahead of the bait. A deep water distance float.*

4. *A 3½ swan reed antenna with cane insert. The sensitive tip clearly shows bites on the drop or lift bites. Bulk shot below halfway.*

5. *A 3½BB cane antenna for short-range fishing in still-water.*

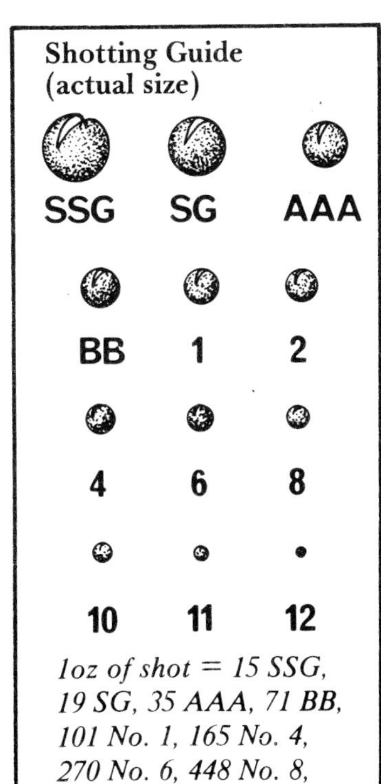

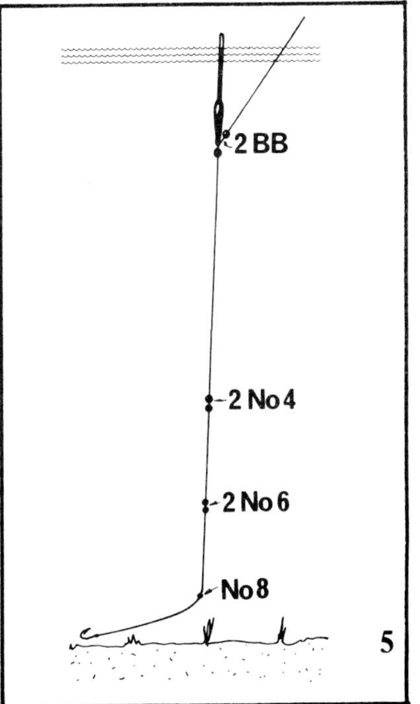

The stick

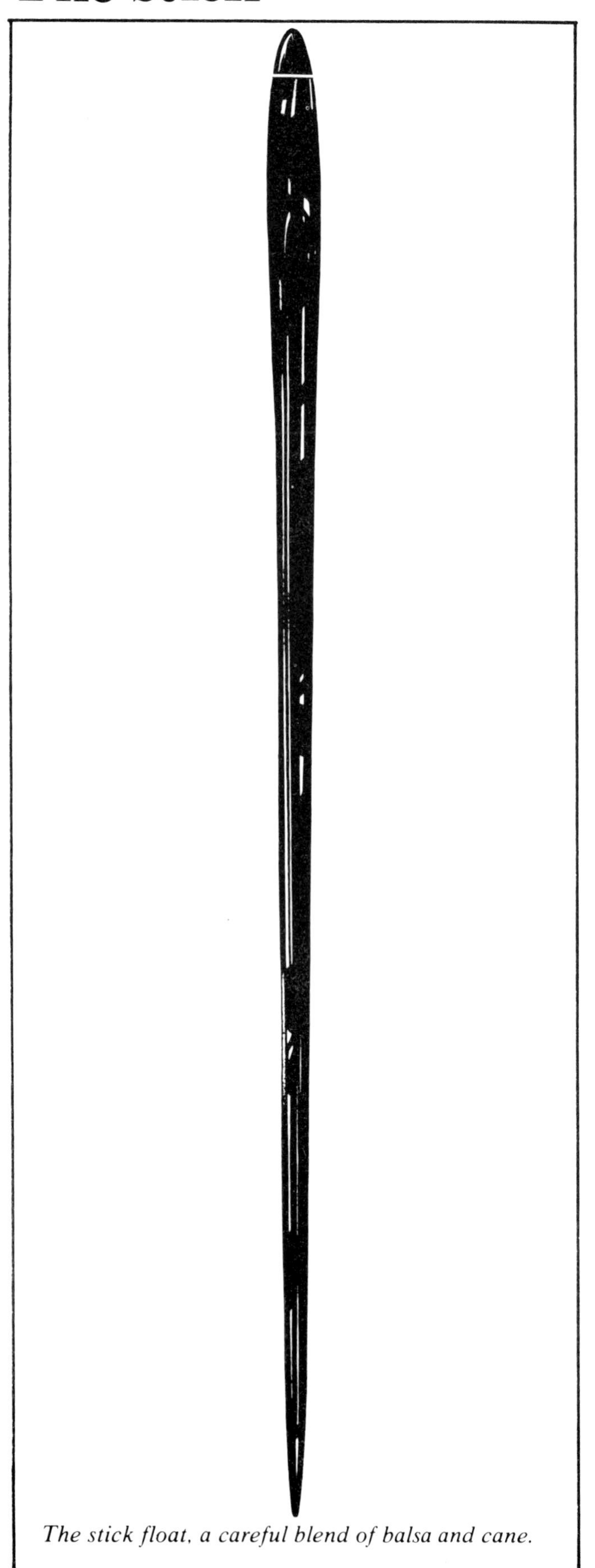
The stick float, a careful blend of balsa and cane.

The delicate stick is the ideal float to use for running water where there is not too much depth, an even glide and a favourable wind.

Originally designed for the Trent by the top North-west anglers, the stick has now found its way into every angler's float box.

Its qualities lie in its ability to carry light shot a fair distance on the cast; cock quickly and show the most delicate bites. Do not use one in a boiling swim or when there is an awkward downstream wind. It must always be fished 'top and bottom'.

Equal balance

The stick's construction is a happy marriage of balsa and cane. The cane at the bottom supplies the weight for casting and encourages the float to sink on a bite. The

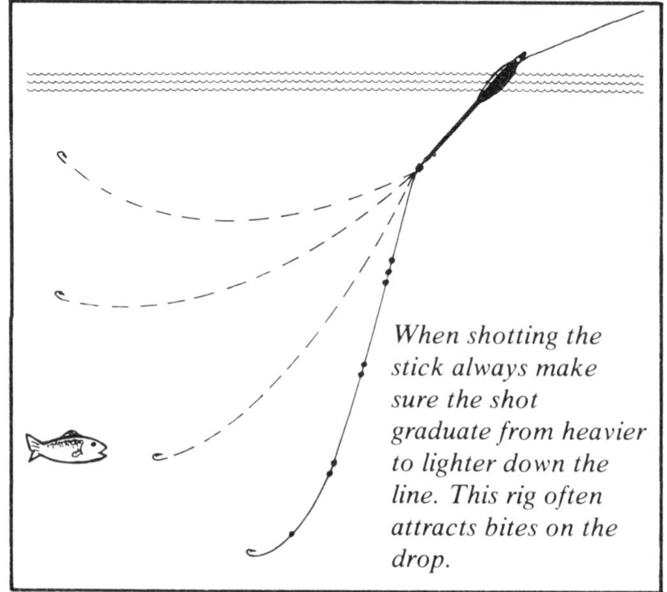
When shotting the stick always make sure the shot graduate from heavier to lighter down the line. This rig often attracts bites on the drop.

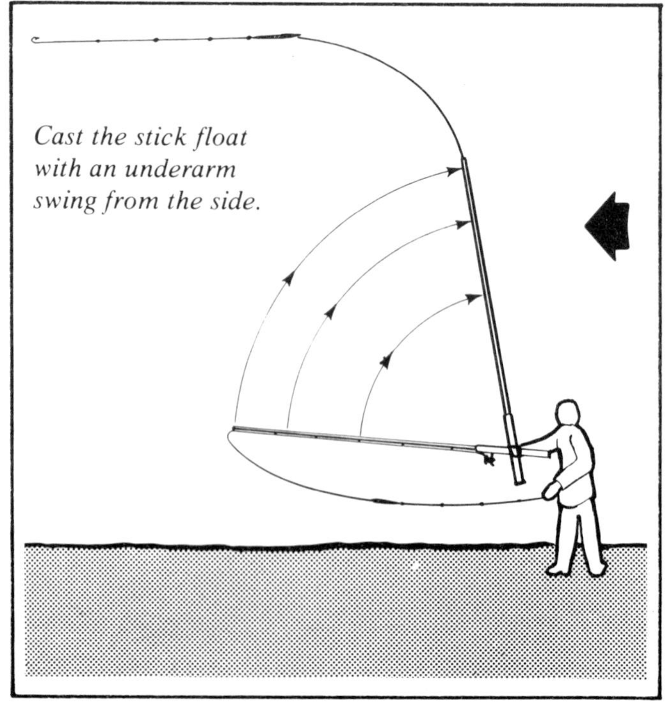
Cast the stick float with an underarm swing from the side.

balsa at the top supplies the buoyancy. The art of making the perfect stick float is to have the two materials balancing equally. As the float cocks, it needs to pivot about this point of balance. If the ratio of materials is wrong, the float cannot be made to work properly—rising out of the water or sinking when either held back or run through.

Stick floats are always fished top and bottom, and shotted down so only the merest dimple shows. Fished bottom end only, the stick float would continually disappear when checked in the swim.

The best way to cast a stick float is an underarm swing from the side. The well-balanced stick will flight perfectly across the water in the horizontal position, allowing the tackle to alight on the surface in a straight line. As the tackle sinks, expect bites on the drop.

Shotting

To allow this delicate presentation, the stick float is shotted up in 'shirt button' style with a shot every foot ranging from a BB under the float to a micro-dust on the hook length. Always make sure the shot graduate from heavier to lighter down the line.

Set the float a foot overdepth, and check its progress as it works its way down the swim. The BB shot under the float will provide the stability; the micro-dust shot near the hook, either a size 8 or 10, will help keep the caster on the bottom. If you have grouped any small shot, these can be moved about to improve bait presentation.

Checking the float will prevent it being dragged under and keep a straight line from rod tip to bait. This way you can literally put the bait right into the fish's mouth.

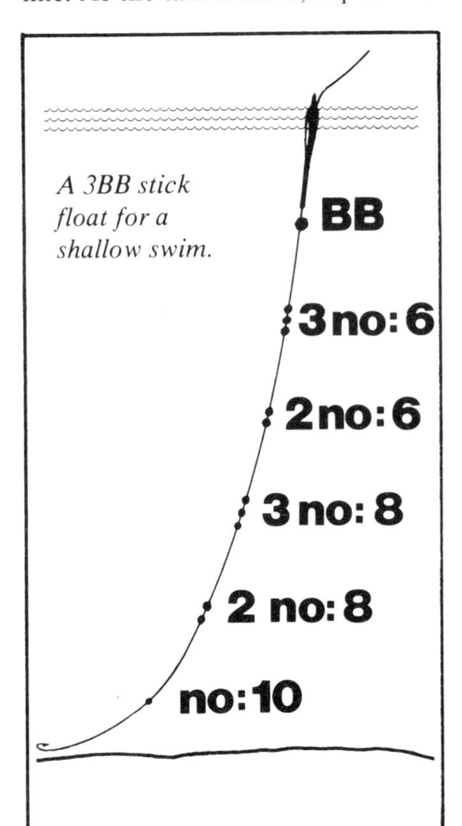

A 3BB stick float for a shallow swim.

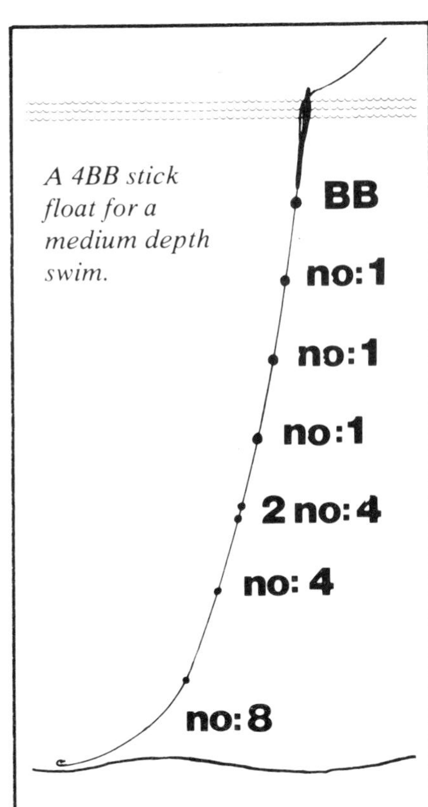

A 4BB stick float for a medium depth swim.

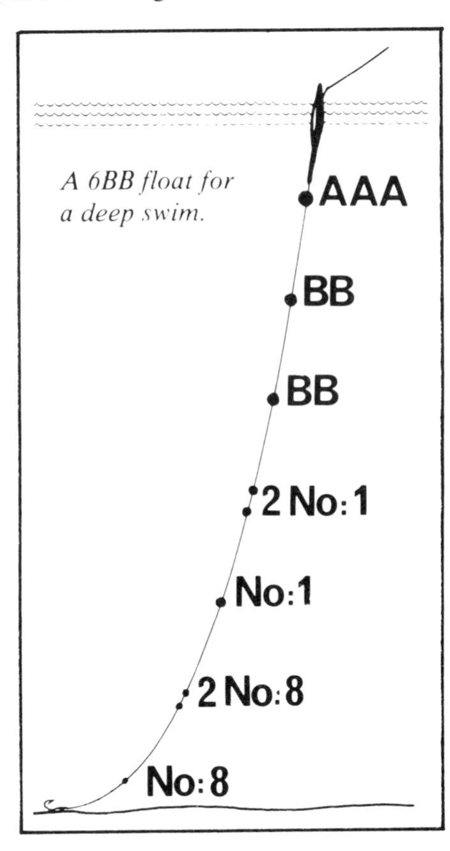

A 6BB float for a deep swim.

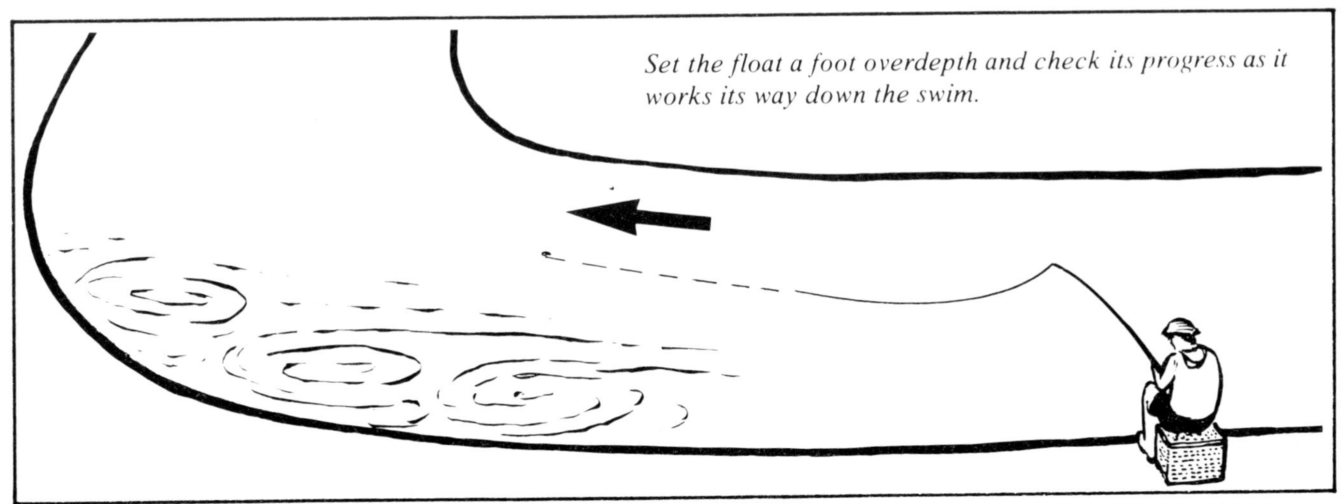
Set the float a foot overdepth and check its progress as it works its way down the swim.

The balsa

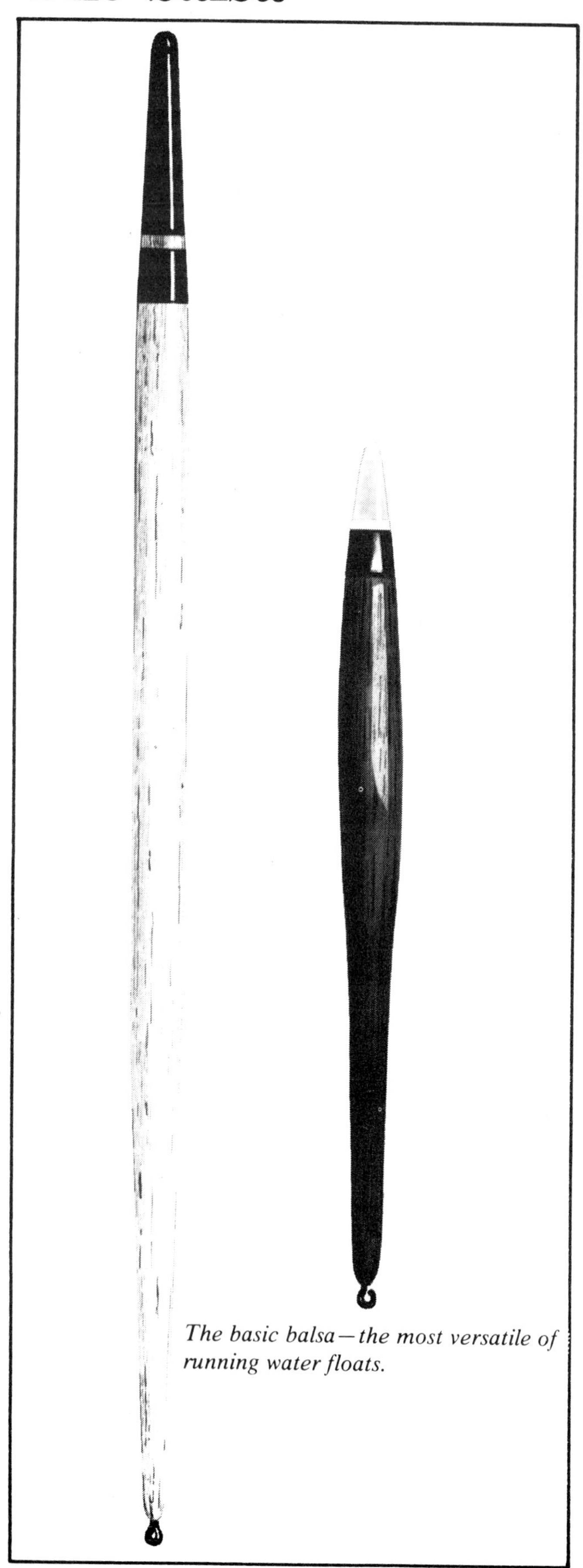

The basic balsa—the most versatile of running water floats.

The simple balsa is the nearest to the all round float for running water. With models available carrying from two BB to four swan, there is no river they cannot tackle.

The balsa performs best in streamy, turbulent water riding strongly through any boils or surface disturbance—conditions where the stick float would be pulled under.

There is no need to guide the balsa through the swim. It confidently makes its own way down the run, gliding with the current past any obstructions. Its buoyancy prevents it being dragged under by the flow.

Small balsas are ideal for stream fishing where the bottom is irregular with boulders pushing the current up to the top. The top Trent matchmen favour tiny balsas for close-in work in fast-water swims. The pointed tops are shotted down and held back on a tight line.

Large baits

For biggish baits such as wasp grub, bread, luncheon meat and worms the larger balsa floats come into their own. Again, they are ideal because of their buoyancy. They hold the bait up in the current and show up at long distances, and also carry plenty of shot for casting.

The balsa range works best on the strong-flowing rivers such as the Hampshire Avon, Trent, Stour, Kennet, Ure, Severn, Wye, Swale, Wharfe or tidal waters. Anywhere where the flow is strong and powerful, the balsa is a useful workhorse.

Shotting

Small balsas can be shotted up in stick float fashion with dust shot placed equally down the line, but on deep, fast water you will need to bulk the shot well down the line to take the bait quickly to the bottom. It may even be necessary to pinch a BB a few inches from the hook. There is no point in using micro-dust on the hooklength when shotting heavy.

The balsa performs well when run through at the same speed as the current, but it can be held back or fished overdepth in quieter water. In fact many top float anglers would say that with a full range of balsas, who needs stick or Avon floats?

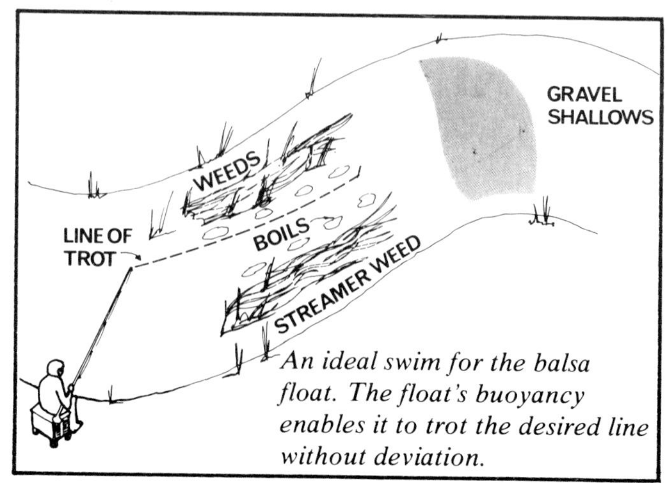

An ideal swim for the balsa float. The float's buoyancy enables it to trot the desired line without deviation.

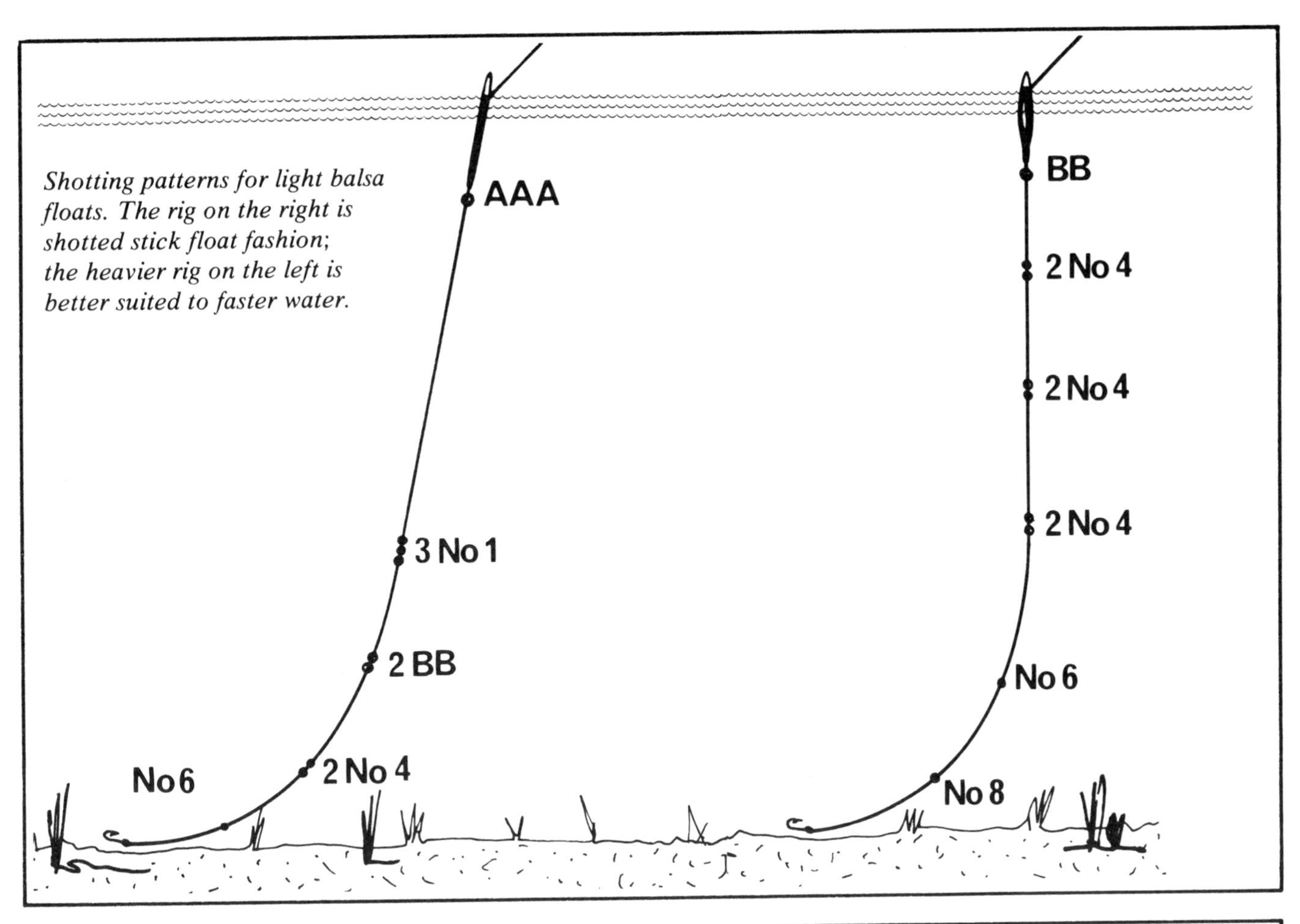

Shotting patterns for light balsa floats. The rig on the right is shotted stick float fashion; the heavier rig on the left is better suited to faster water.

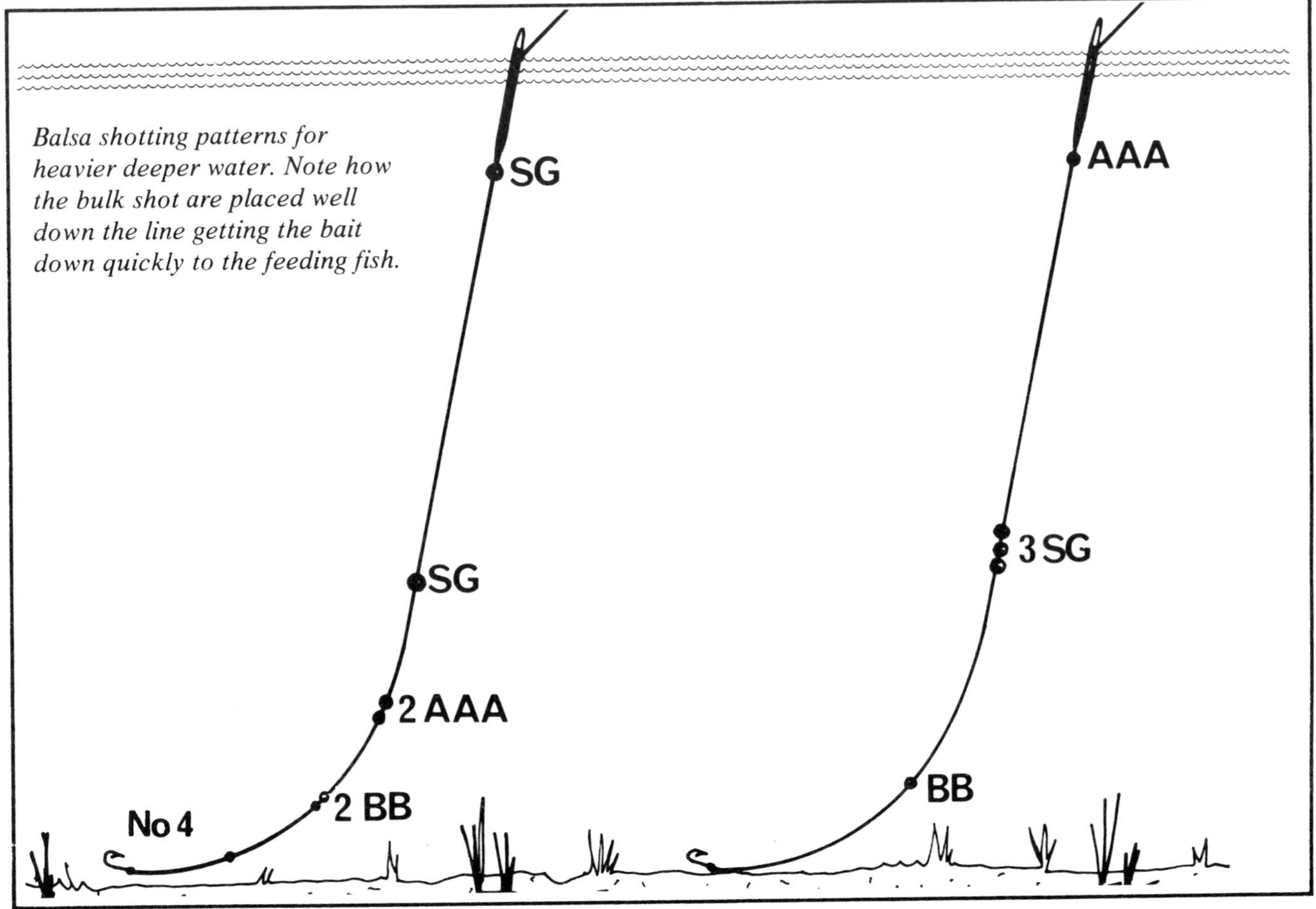

Balsa shotting patterns for heavier deeper water. Note how the bulk shot are placed well down the line getting the bait down quickly to the feeding fish.

Sliding floats

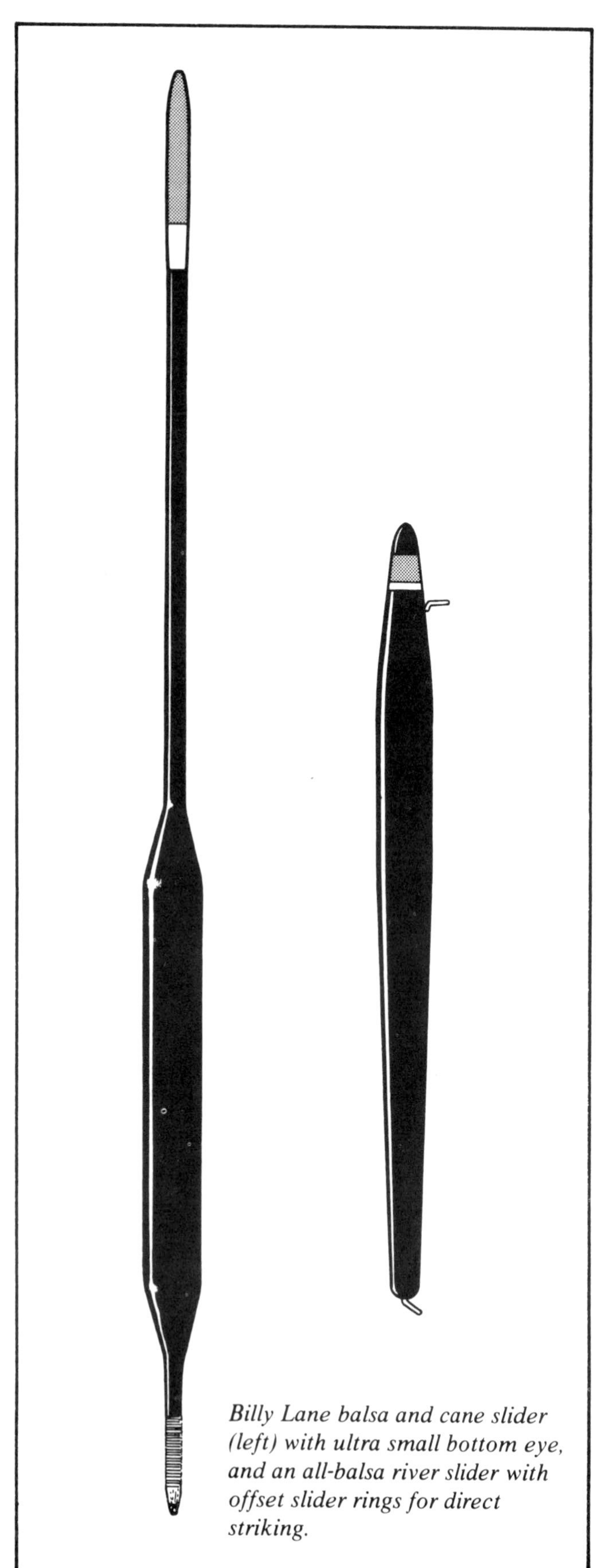

Billy Lane balsa and cane slider (left) with ultra small bottom eye, and an all-balsa river slider with offset slider rings for direct striking.

The slider is feared and misunderstood by many anglers, so much so that very few even carry one in their otherwise bulging float boxes. Faced with a swim deeper than the length of their rod, many plump for the leger and throw away the possibility of a good catch by using the slider.

Even in deep swims, fish are not always hugging the bottom. The bomb will only scantily search out the last few feet whereas the slider, if correctly shotted, will find fish from the surface right down to the bottom.

Sliders have the distinct advantage over all other floats in that the shotting pattern is almost invariably the same. Only the size of the shot is altered to match the different floats. Many anglers find the slider rig very prone to tangling on the cast but this can be overcome if the float is cast underhand and if possible into the wind.

Float characteristics

To get the best from a slider you must study how the float behaves as it settles. When it reaches the water, the float will lie flat until the stop knot reaches the tiny eye. This means that the heavy bulk shot will have reached

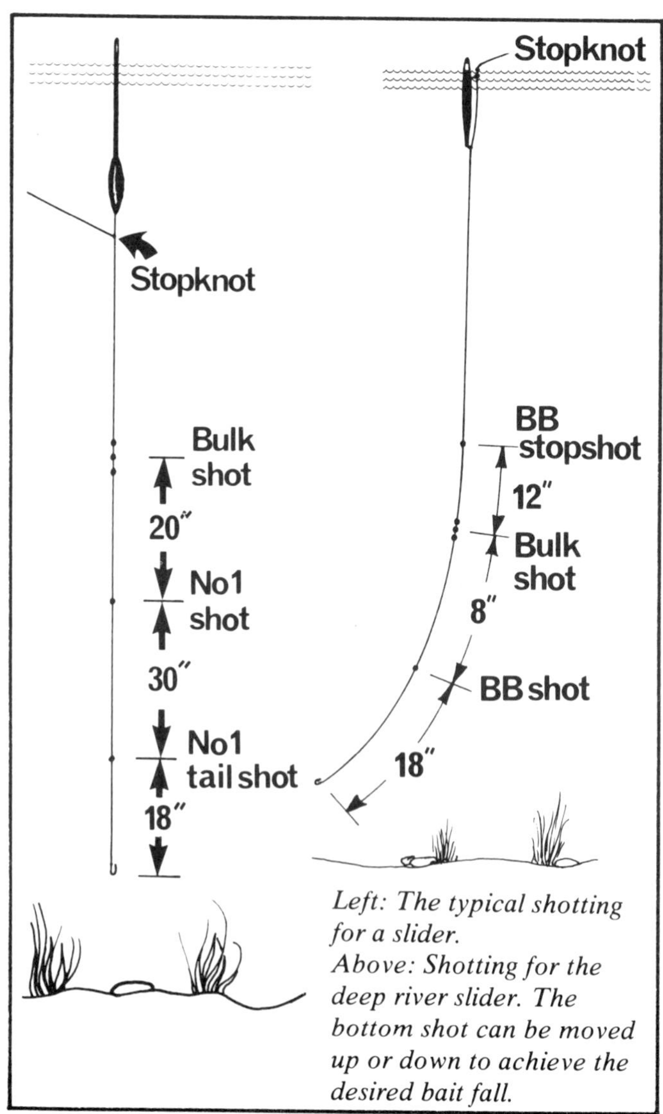

Left: The typical shotting for a slider.
Above: Shotting for the deep river slider. The bottom shot can be moved up or down to achieve the desired bait fall.

full depth making the float suddenly jerk upright, but still leaving most of the antenna showing.

The next shot will then find its own maximum depth and will take the float down even further.

The last shot is now on its way down to register the final float setting, leaving the tip between half and one inch above the surface.

A fish may intercept the bait in between shot settling times, leaving the float higher in the water for longer than normal. Or the float may show a distinct lift as a fish takes the bait and swims upwards. The final and more usual indication is when the float sinks to a bottom-feeding fish.

Sliders are usually set to fish just off the bottom but they will also fish a bait on the bottom. To shot up for this method, slide the last shot to 20 inches from the hook, the next shot a further three feet and the bulk shot the same again. In some cases this will put the bulk loading very close to the float, in effect turning the slider into a zoomer.

Sliders can also be very effective in running water but the usual antenna sort must be changed for a two-ringed float made from a stout bird quill or balsa. Both the rings should be offset from the float so that the reel line simply drops through these rings.

This slider is useful when deep swims cannot be mastered with a normal float fixed at full depth because bankside trees hamper accurate casting.

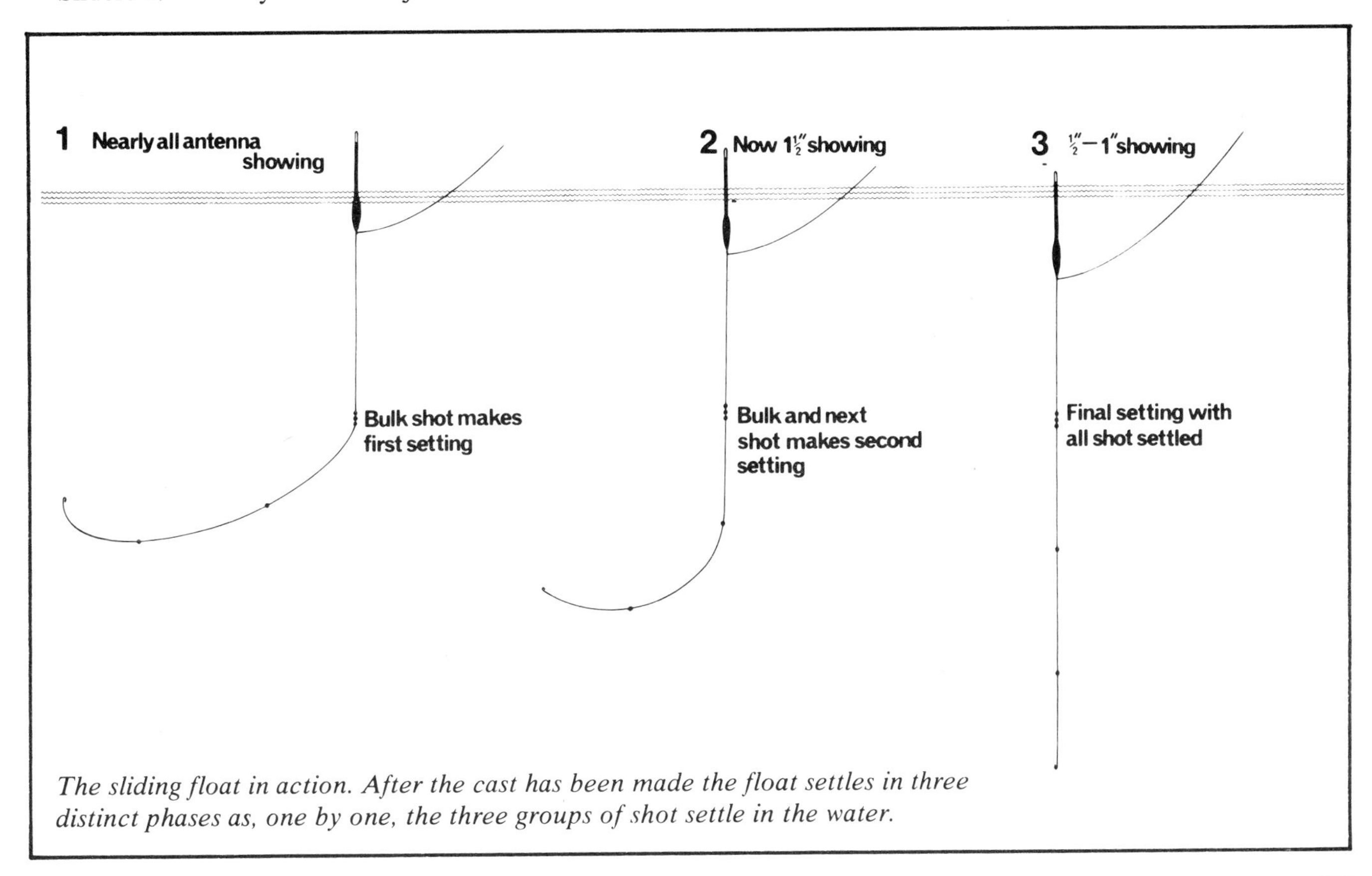

The sliding float in action. After the cast has been made the float settles in three distinct phases as, one by one, the three groups of shot settle in the water.

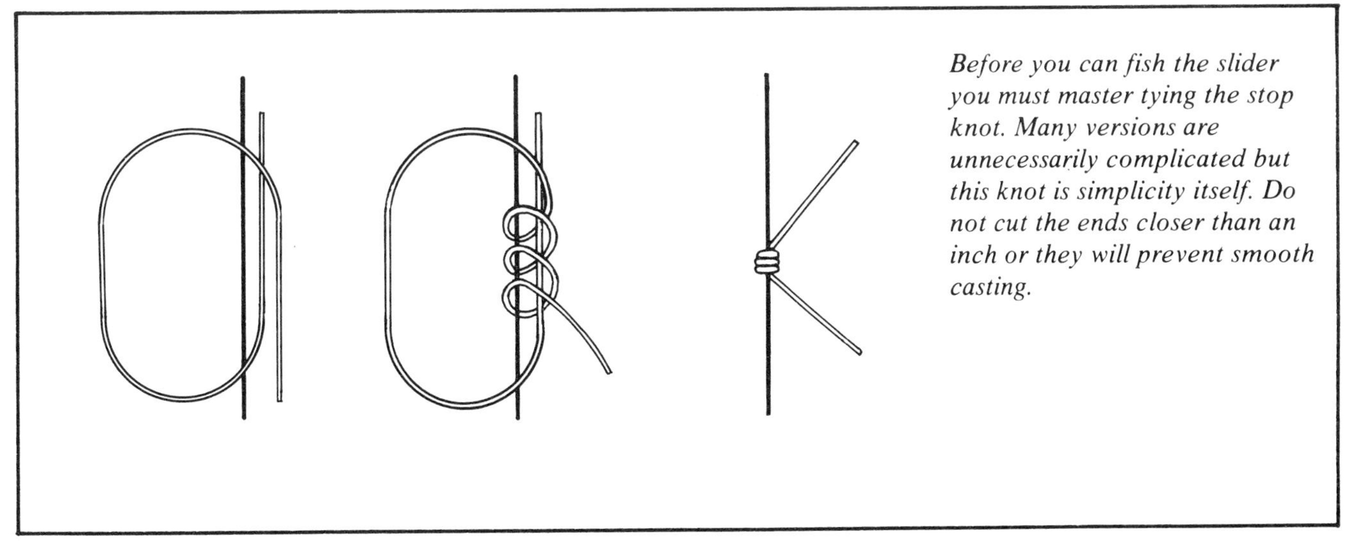
Before you can fish the slider you must master tying the stop knot. Many versions are unnecessarily complicated but this knot is simplicity itself. Do not cut the ends closer than an inch or they will prevent smooth casting.

Legering

During the last two decades the art of legering has been transformed from a crude, hit-or-miss affair to one of the most sophisticated and deadly methods of catching fish.

The transformation is entirely due to the invention of simple, yet effective bite indicators, originally developed by top matchmen. Legering will catch fish on days when floatfishing is virtually impossible. The method should not be dismissed as a last ditch technique, however. Under the right conditions it can be even more effective than fishing with a float.

Legering is simply the art of fishing without a float. Many of the old methods of bite indication, the dough bobbin, and rod top legering can still be used today. However, except under certain conditions they are far less effective than modern techniques.

Tackle

Rods It is pointless to use an ordinary 12 or 13 foot float rod for legering. A specialist rod is essential. Ideally the angler should have two leger rods—one for swingtipping, the other for quiver-tipping. But for the general angler or beginner, a single rod will be sufficient. The leger rod must be balanced to line strength in exactly the same way as the float rod. It must be capable of casting 30 yards or more with up to $\frac{3}{4}$oz of lead, and picking up the same amount of line on the strike without causing line breakage. Like the float rod it should be correctly ringed and have an all-through rather than a tip action.

The ideal rod length is around 9 feet 6 inches. If it is shorter the angler will experience difficulty in picking up line quickly; and if it is longer he will have difficulty in studying the movements of his swingtip or quivertip which is attached to the end of the rod.

Reels Centre pin reels are useless for legering but the fixed spool reels used for float fishing are ideal. Remember to fill the spool correctly to within $\frac{1}{8}$ of an inch of the spool lip to obtain maximum casting distance.

Lines There is no need to use a heavy line when legering—unless you are expecting to catch big fish like barbel or big chub. A line in the $2\frac{1}{2}$lb range is ideal but it needs to be one that will sink quickly. Lines can be made to sink for legering by soaking overnight in washing-up liquid. This treatment does tend to rot a line in time so always check your legering line carefully.

Bite indicators

The introduction of the swingtip revolutionised legering. The swingtip is merely a short piece of cane or stiff nylon with two rings whipped to it that is either permanently lashed to the rod or screwed in to a special end ring adapter now fitted to most mass produced leger rods. A small section of silicone, or valve, rubber acts as a hinge between rod tip and swingtip allowing the swingtip to hang at right angles to the rod. The line is threaded through the rod rings and the rings of the swingtip in the normal way. After casting the rod should be put in a rod rest at an angle of 45 degrees to the bank and the line tightened to the lead so that the swingtip is under some tension. Bites will be signalled by the swingtip lifting or dropping back. The length of the swingtip is important. A long swingtip, up to 12 inches, takes less effort to move than a short one and is better suited to windy conditions.

The swingtip is best suited to still or slow moving waters. In a strong current it will tend to pull out verti-

The start of the strike when legering. Note how the rod has been set up almost parallel to the river. When a bite is indicated the rod is lifted slightly and swept backwards with a flat steady sweep of the right arm. The left hand is placed on the reel handle giving the angler instant contact at all times with the hooked fish.

cally, making bites difficult to spot. Although lead wire can be wound round its tip ring to counteract this movement, it does reduce its effectiveness and it is time to switch to the quivertip.

The quivertip is screwed into the end of the leger rod in the same way as the swingtip. It is simply a thin tapered piece of fibreglass, up to 10 inches long and ideal for legering in flowing water. The position of the rings on the quivertip is vital. They must be placed so that when the line is tightened to the lead, the quivertip assumes the correct curve.

After casting, the rod is again put in the rests at an

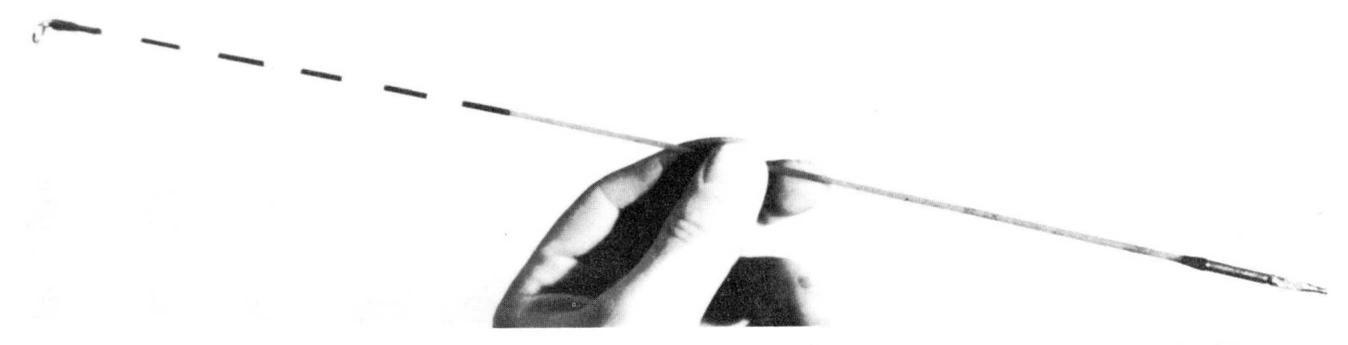

The quivertip is really a more sophisticated form of the old, crude method of simply watching the rod tip for bites. The quivertip screws into the end of the rod tip.

The swingtip set up for action. The fish on the right will pick up the bait and swim away from the angler, with the swingtip signalling a bite by lifting upwards. The fish on the left will swim towards the angler causing the swingtip to drop back towards the water.

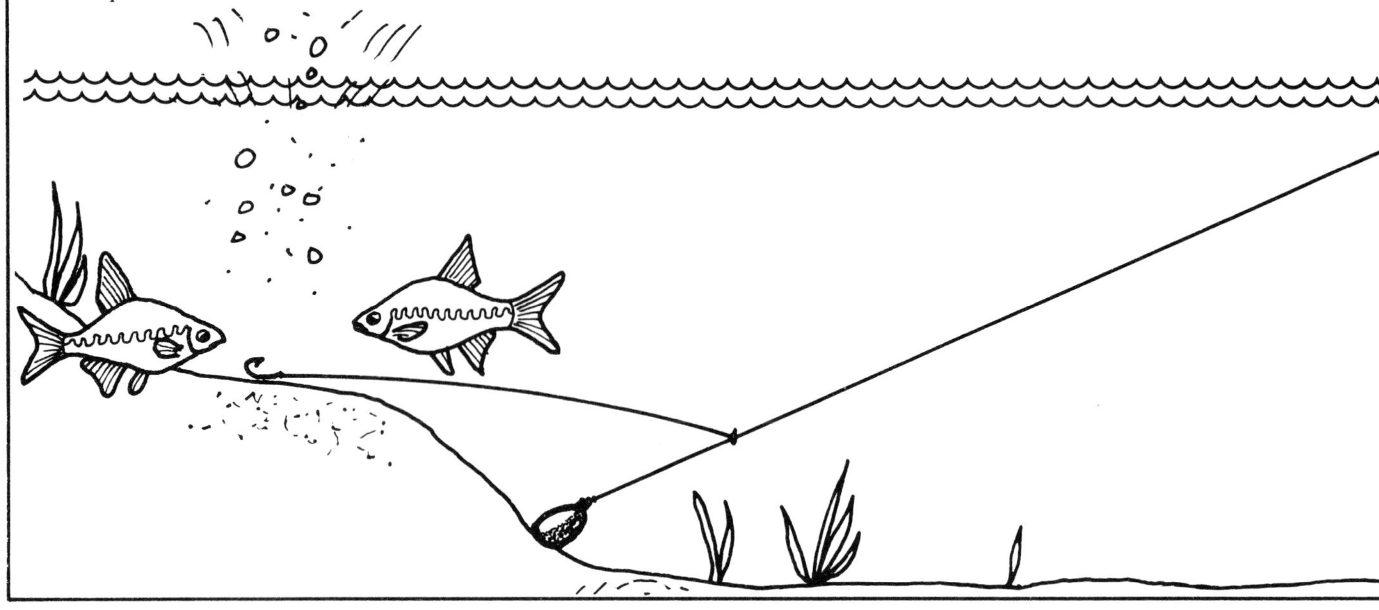

angle of 45 degrees to the bank or parallel to the bank. The quivertip will assume a natural curve and bites will be signalled by the quivertip pulling round towards the river or dropping back.

One vital point when fishing with quivertip or swingtip on flowing water is to position the rod tip in the direction of the flow. With the rod pointing downstream the angler is in direct contact with his fish when striking. Point the rod upstream and a bow of line will form underwater making it more difficult to strike directly into a fish.

The method of striking is important too. Never strike upwards when swingtipping or quivertipping. The water resistance to the line will make the strike ineffective. Strike sideways to lessen resistance and you will hook more fish.

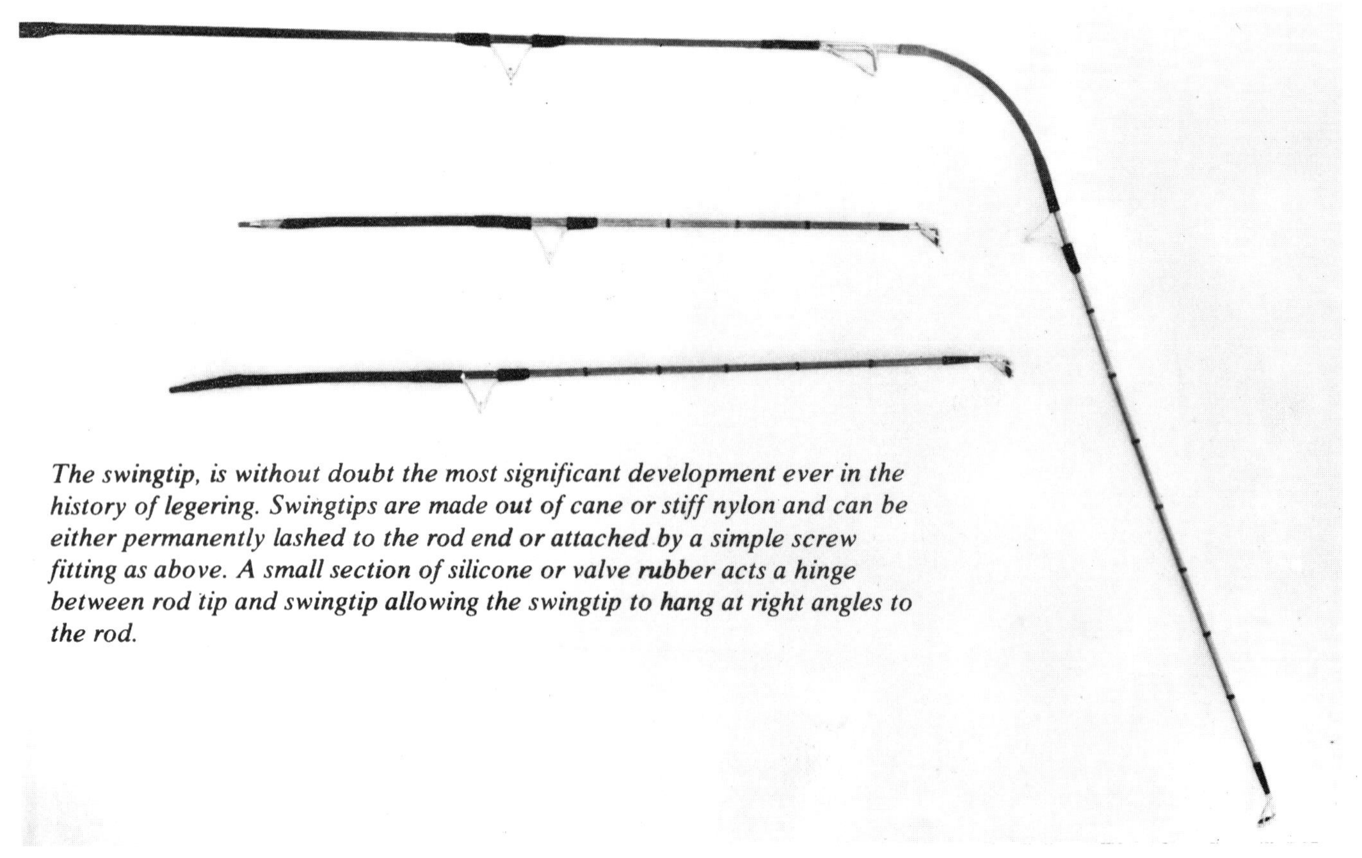

The swingtip, is without doubt the most significant development ever in the history of legering. Swingtips are made out of cane or stiff nylon and can be either permanently lashed to the rod end or attached by a simple screw fitting as above. A small section of silicone or valve rubber acts a hinge between rod tip and swingtip allowing the swingtip to hang at right angles to the rod.

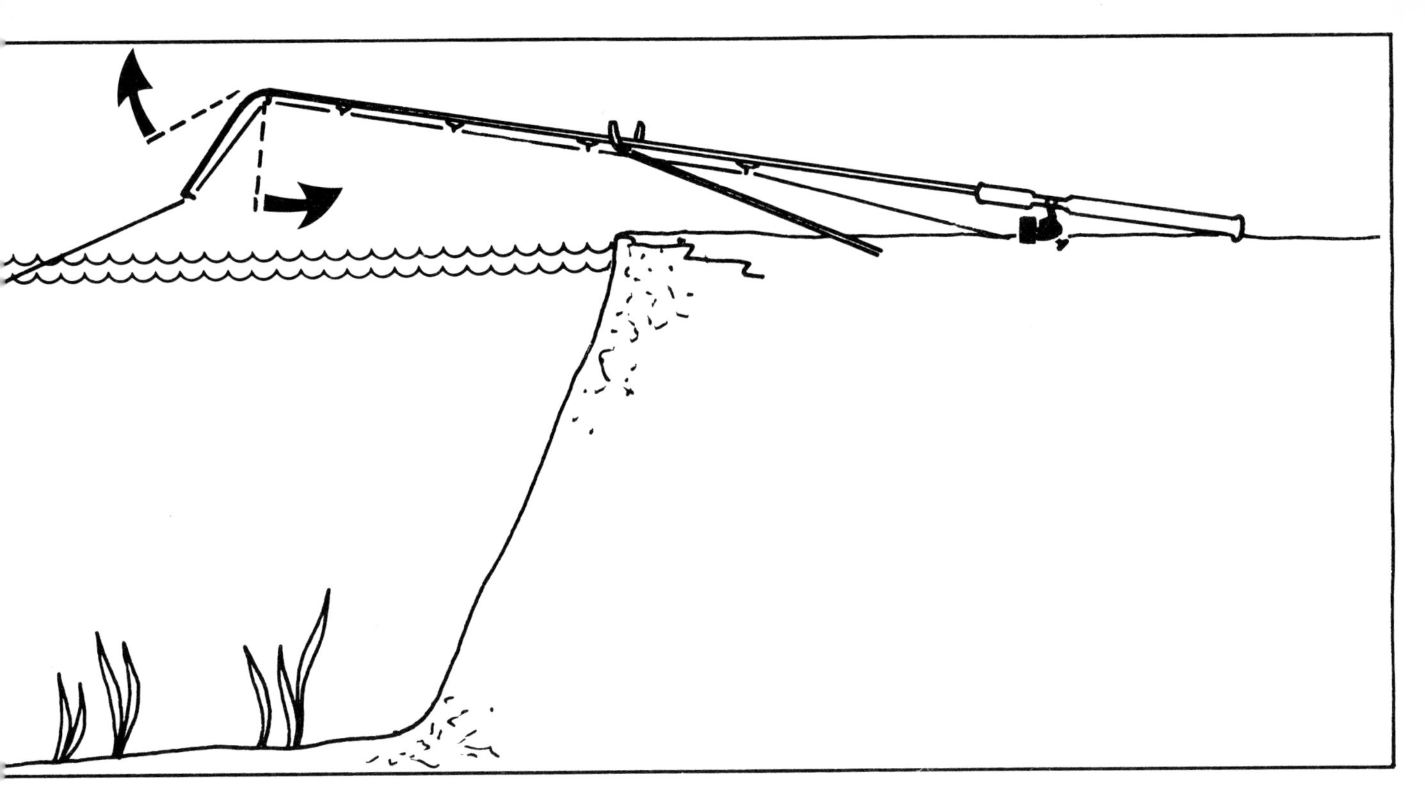

Butt indicators

For stillwater fishing the butt bite indicator is another useful weapon in the leger angler's armoury. The indicator consists of a Terry clip, a valve rubber pivot and a short arm of either stiff wire, glass or cane with an end ring. The indicator is clipped to the rod, usually just above the butt joint and the line threaded through the indicator arm ring and then through the rod rings. After casting the line is tightened so the indicator is under tension at an angle of about 45 degrees.

Bites will be signalled by the arm lifting towards the rod or dropping back. Unlike the swingtip or quivertip the rod tip must always be pointed directly at the lead at right angles to the bank.

The butt indicator really comes into its own on windy days when the swingtip and quivertip are blown about. The rod tip can be sunk and the butt indicator protected from any side wind by the angler's umbrella. There is no need to have a special leger rod when using the butt indicator as your normal float rod will do.

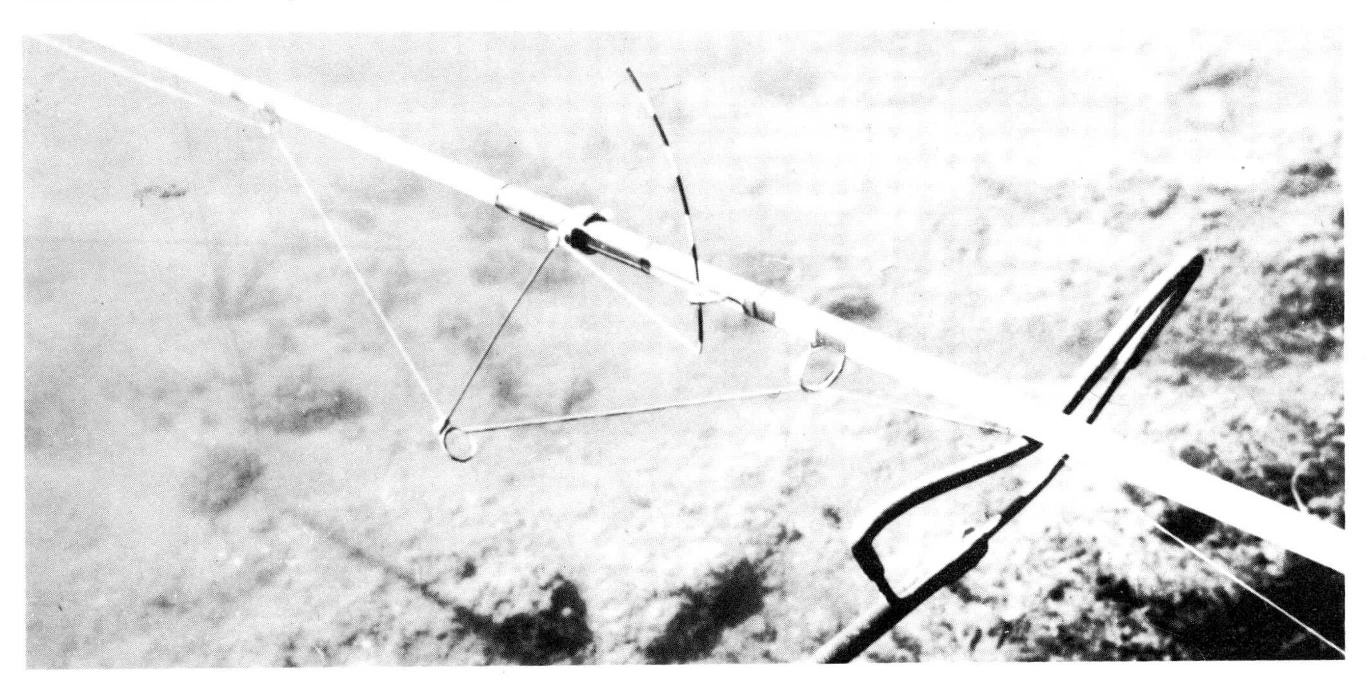

A sophisticated form of butt indicator with the angler watching the movement of the black and white arm for indication of bites. Indicators such as these are deadly on windy days but are not suited to fast flowing waters.

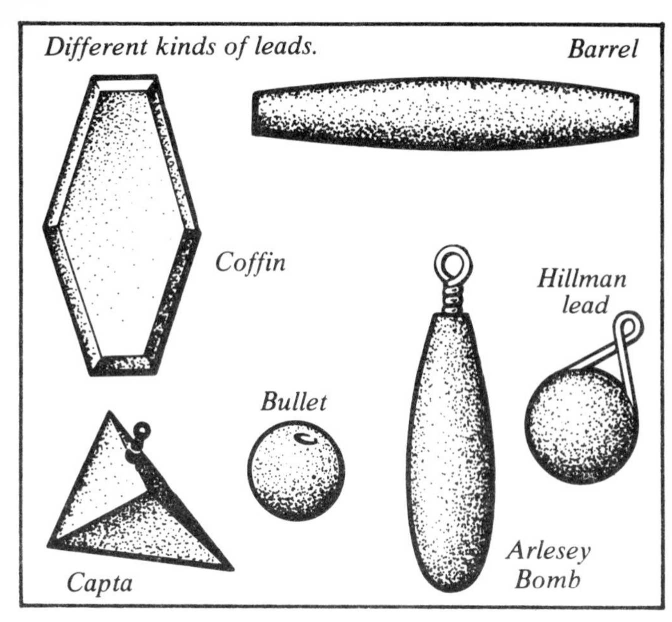

Different kinds of leads.

Leads

The most widely used leads are the drilled bullet and the Arlesey bomb. For rolling a bait for big fish through a fast-moving swim the drilled bullet is ideal. They can be bought from any tackle shop, in a variety of different weights and are simply threaded on the line and stopped anything from six to 18 inches from the hook by a split shot.

The swan shot link leger can also be used effectively under the same conditions. Simply pinch a few swan shot on a separate loop of line and leave a hole small enough at the top of the loop so that an AAA stop shot does not slide through.

Arlesey bombs, although they can be used for fast water fishing are more widely used for legering on still or slow moving waters. Never thread them on the line like a drilled bullet, they work more effectively when fished on a paternoster link. Simply tie the hook to the

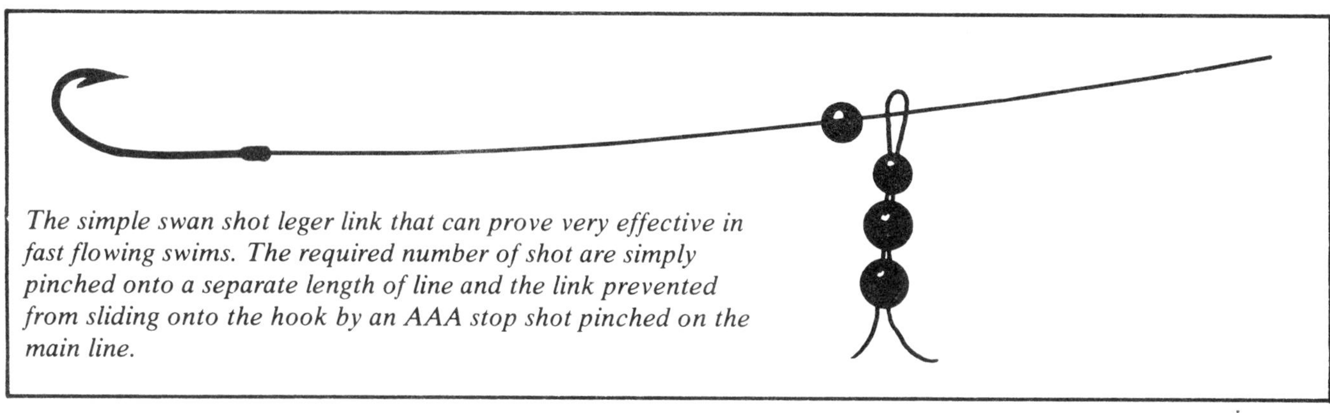

The simple swan shot leger link that can prove very effective in fast flowing swims. The required number of shot are simply pinched onto a separate length of line and the link prevented from sliding onto the hook by an AAA stop shot pinched on the main line.

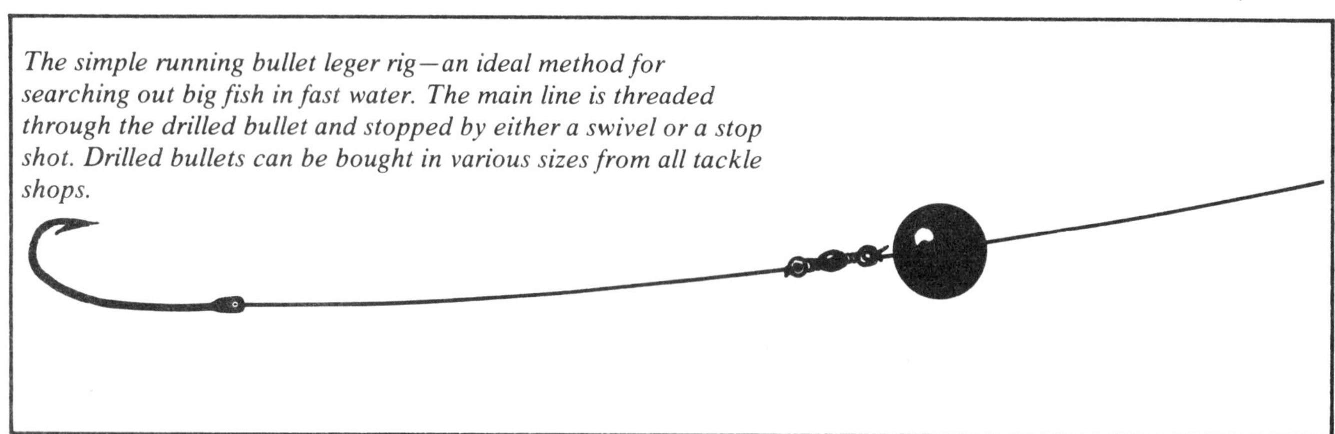

The simple running bullet leger rig—an ideal method for searching out big fish in fast water. The main line is threaded through the drilled bullet and stopped by either a swivel or a stop shot. Drilled bullets can be bought in various sizes from all tackle shops.

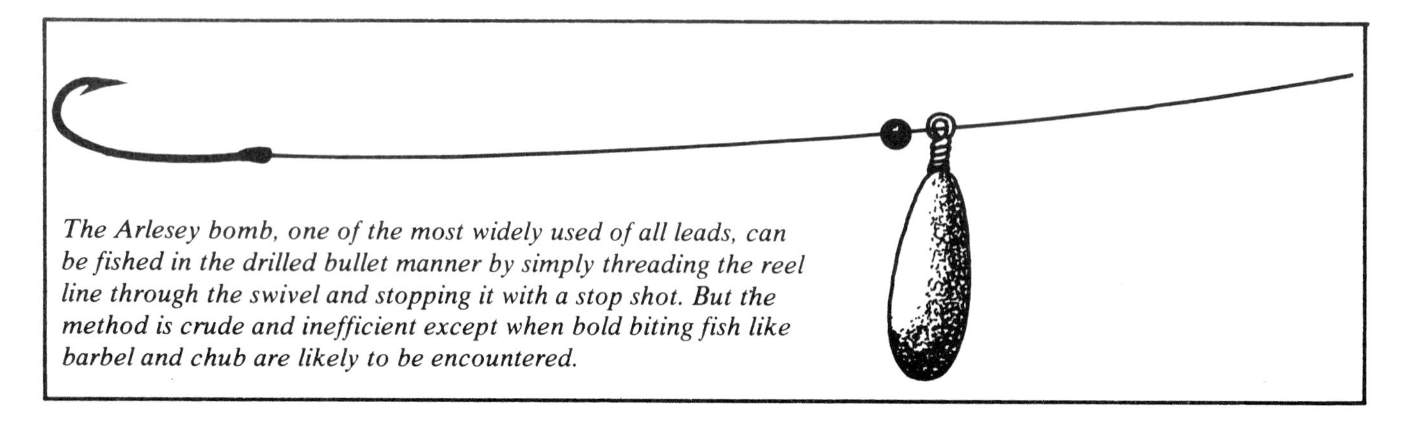

The Arlesey bomb, one of the most widely used of all leads, can be fished in the drilled bullet manner by simply threading the reel line through the swivel and stopping it with a stop shot. But the method is crude and inefficient except when bold biting fish like barbel and chub are likely to be encountered.

end of the reel line in the normal way; take a short piece of nylon and tie it on to the reel line with a water knot. Then tie the Arlesey bomb to this link, which should be about nine inches long.

Water conditions and the species the angler expects to catch will dictate the length of 'tail'—the distance between the paternoster link and the hook. The greater the distance, the slower the fall of the bait through the water after casting.

In summer, when the fish are more likely to be in midwater, a long tail, up to five feet, will be more effective. In winter when the fish will be found on the river bed, a short tail of 2½–3 feet will produce more bites. If you are legering and getting bites which produce no indication on your swingtip or quivertip, shorten your tail immediately until a definite registration is shown. If you are getting no bites at all try lengthening the tail. Never be afraid to experiment.

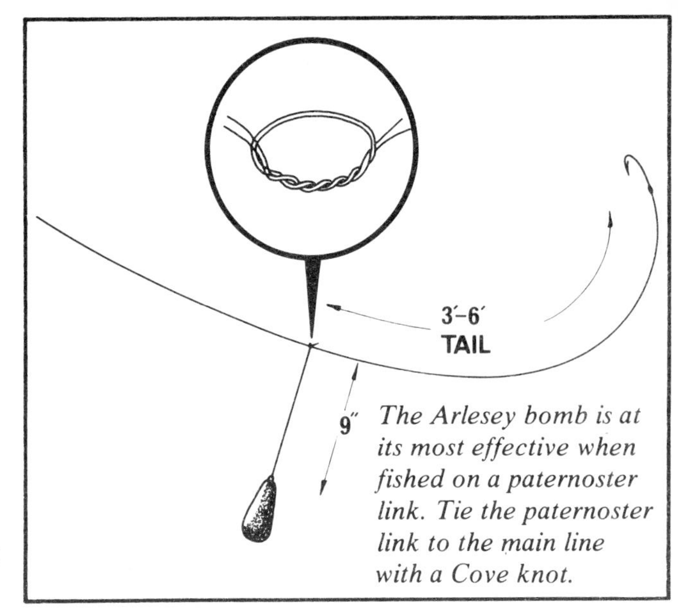

The Arlesey bomb is at its most effective when fished on a paternoster link. Tie the paternoster link to the main line with a Cove knot.

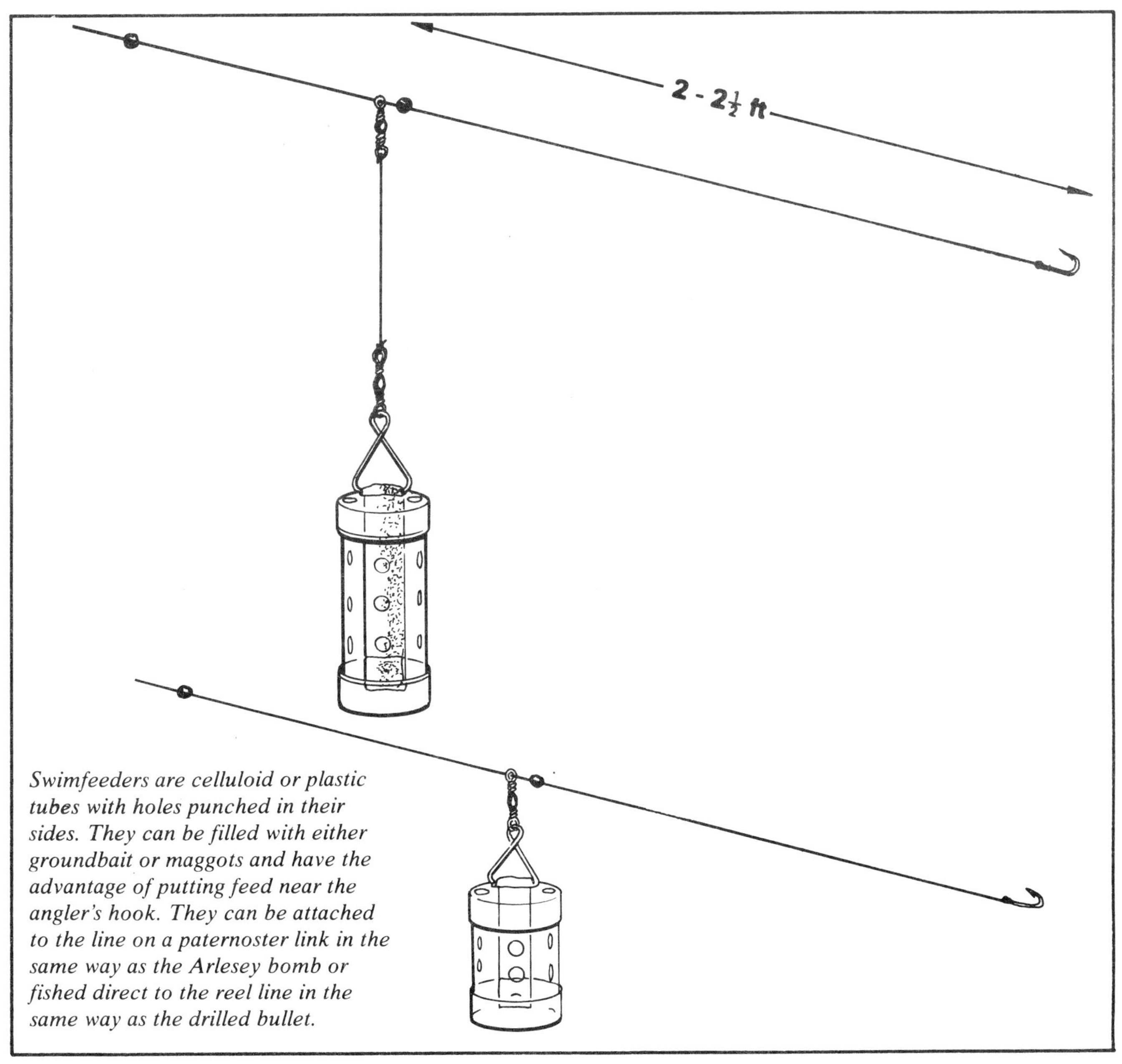

Swimfeeders are celluloid or plastic tubes with holes punched in their sides. They can be filled with either groundbait or maggots and have the advantage of putting feed near the angler's hook. They can be attached to the line on a paternoster link in the same way as the Arlesey bomb or fished direct to the reel line in the same way as the drilled bullet.

Two basic knots

The Cove knot is one of the simplest yet most useful knots in angling. It can be used in trout fishing for attaching leaders with, or without droppers, and in legering for attaching a paternoster bomb link to the main reel line. It is very easy to tie—a vital factor in blustery winds or on bitter winter days when the angler's fingers are numb with cold!

In most types of coarse fishing the business end of the tackle, the hook length, is the most vital few inches of all.

Most anglers use a finer breaking strain hook length than reel line. The junction of the two can often be a weak link. Joining the two together by loops is one answer. But the double loops do tend to collect rubbish. The blood knot is another alternative but one that is often unreliable when different strength lines are being joined together.

The Cove knot

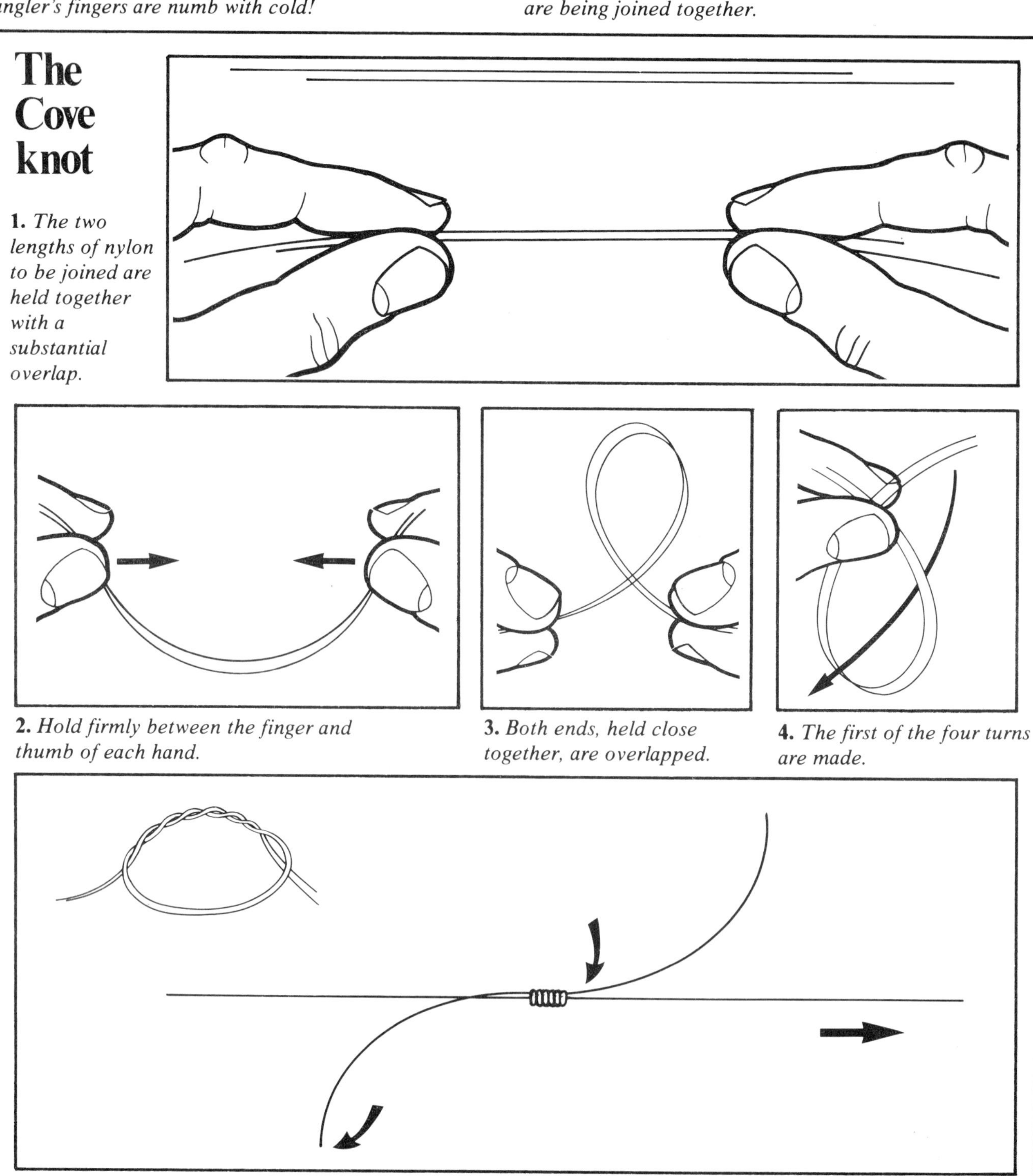

1. *The two lengths of nylon to be joined are held together with a substantial overlap.*

2. *Hold firmly between the finger and thumb of each hand.*

3. *Both ends, held close together, are overlapped.*

4. *The first of the four turns are made.*

5. *The loose turns are moistened and drawn together. For trout fishing the end pointing up the cast can be left as a dropper. For legering tie the bomb to one end and snip the other close to the knot.*

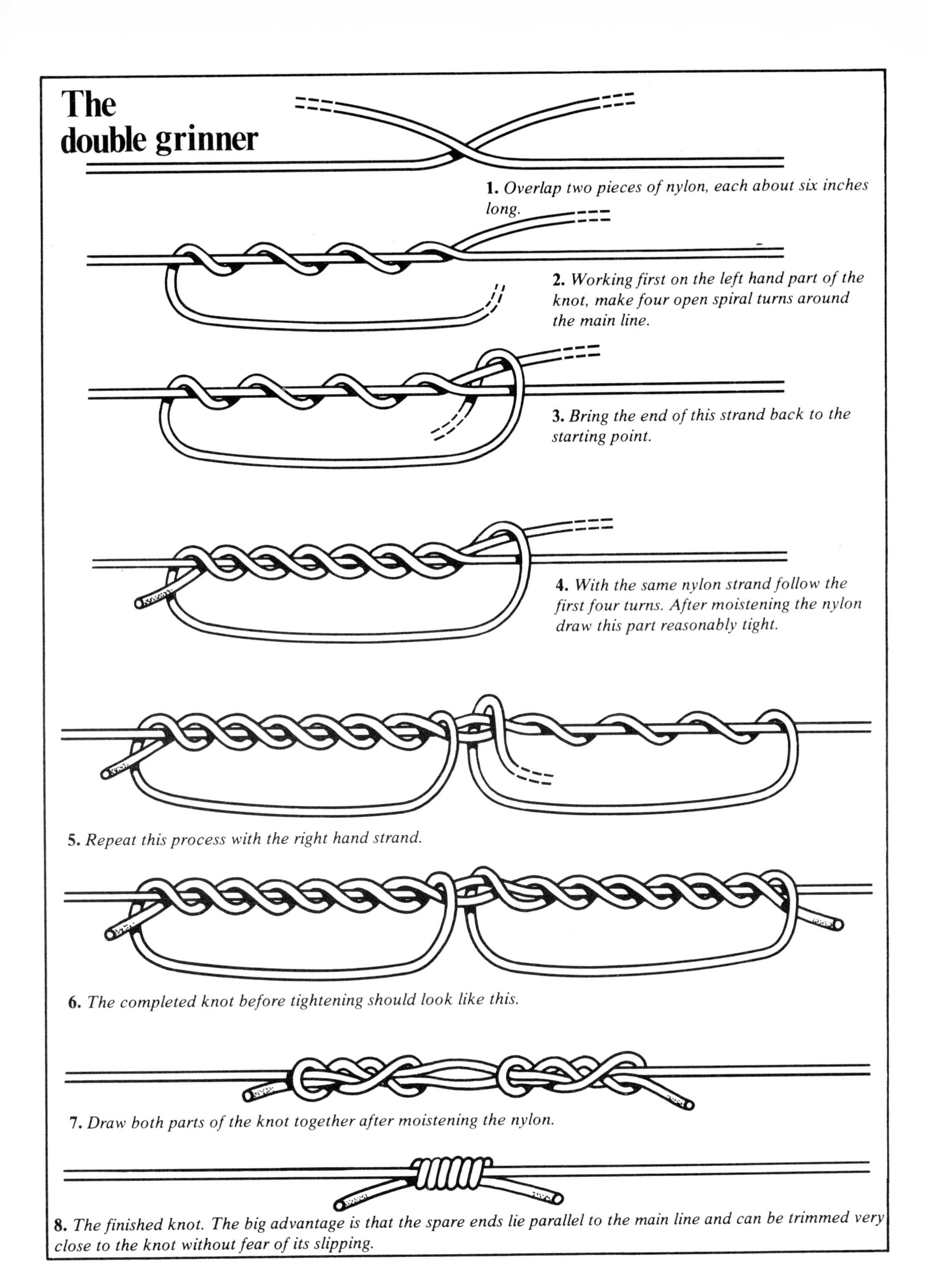
The double grinner
1. Overlap two pieces of nylon, each about six inches long.
2. Working first on the left hand part of the knot, make four open spiral turns around the main line.
3. Bring the end of this strand back to the starting point.
4. With the same nylon strand follow the first four turns. After moistening the nylon draw this part reasonably tight.
5. Repeat this process with the right hand strand.
6. The completed knot before tightening should look like this.
7. Draw both parts of the knot together after moistening the nylon.
8. The finished knot. The big advantage is that the spare ends lie parallel to the main line and can be trimmed very close to the knot without fear of its slipping.

Roach

Ask any coarse fisherman his favourite fish and nine out of ten will name the roach. Silvery-scaled with a tinge of blue, scarlet-finned and vermilion-red, the handsome roach is a fish to be admired. It's not all show either, for the roach has a cunning to match its sharp appearance. Delicate tackle well presented is needed to bring the bites. The ultra-fine technique of roach poles and dainty crow quills was developed by the London anglers to fool the shy roach of the Thames and its tributaries. Then followed the Sheffield style of the Northern matchmen—light floats and centre-pin reels.

Whatever style you adopt—and there are many that will take roach—this sought-after species will give you many hours of enjoyable fishing. Catching a good bag of average roach is always fun, and a really big specimen can only be described as the ultimate thrill for anglers.

No record fish has caused more excitement than the recent top roach. It always has been, and always will be, the record that every angler would like to hold.

Techniques

The roach is a delicate feeder, so your tackle must allow for this. There is often no need to fish far out. The fish will be in the side, provided there is some cover.

For general river fishing the stick float takes some beating. Made from cane and balsa, it is ideal for smooth running water where the bait needs to be tripping along the bottom. The best way to fish this float—especially in winter—is to hold the float back in the current so that the bait travels down slower than the stream. This way the fish have no need to chase after the bait, and can take it in while still maintaining their position in the current.

The stick float is the modern replacement for the more traditional crow and porcupine quill floats. But these floats still have their uses, especially in shallow water. When the current is stronger and more turbulent such as on rivers like the Hampshire Avon, or the Severn, then you will need an all-balsa float that will not be pulled under the current. This float will take more shot, which you will need to take your bait down to the fish.

On the wider, deeper rivers such as the Thames or Nene you may need to fish at distance. For this you can use one of the many hundred of different antenna, or waggler, floats. The buoyant balsa body at the base of the float is to defeat the effects of wind and drag. The thin stem is made from peacock quill or sarkandas reed.

These floats are attached by the bottom ring only, and the line sunk beneath the surface to beat the wind. With shot pinched round the float, this gives you the weight for casting. As the rest of the shot fall slowly through the water, look for roach bites 'on the drop'. If the float fails to settle in the water to cover the white ring, then it is likely that a fish has taken the bait during its descent. For this style a cane inset in the float's tip gives more sensitivity. It is not so buoyant as peacock and goes under or pops up easier. If there is a current, the float will move through the water ahead of the bait once it has reached the bottom—the opposite of the stick float. A fish intercepting the bait will make the float disappear without the fish moving its position.

If the current's strong, you can still use this type of float, but you will not want a cane inset. Just remove a small shot to allow more tip to show. Then slightly hold back the line as it travels through the water. The buoyant peacock quill tip will prevent the float being dragged under, except on a bite.

This is the waggler style, deadly on rivers such as the Trent and Warwickshire Avon. And the float is also useful for lakes and gravel pits where you need to cast some distance.

For narrower still waters such as canals or drains small antennas such as the dart come into their own with dust shot spaced down the line.

For roach, always remember to fish as light as conditions will allow. Hook lengths need not be more than 1½lb. But while pinkie maggots demand a size 20 hook, a piece of flake or cheese may need a size 10.

Location

The roach is the most widespread of all our freshwater fish being found from Scottish lochs to West Country game rivers and it can tolerate a fair degree of pollution.

Before disease decimated the shoals in the 1960s, the largest roach caught came from the London reservoirs, or the Hampshire and Wiltshire chalk streams such as the Avon, Kennet, Wylye and Nadder. These clear waters were rich in food such as shrimps and snails and the fish grew deep and fat. London angler Bill Penney took his record roach in 1938 from Lambeth Reservoir, while five years before a roach of 3lb 10oz had come from the Hampshire Avon.

Today the reservoirs are largely empty of roach while big fish are few and far between in the chalk rivers. But the species is making a strong revival, especially in the East of England.

Roach have returned in force to the Fenland drains,

while winter fishing on the lower reaches of the Lincolnshire's River Welland is second to none. The Nene provides good sport with roach in autumn while the Great Ouse in the Ely area is another noted winter hotspot.

Norfolk's famous roach rivers—the Bure, Wensum and Waveney—are slowly returning to form with two-pounders every season. Again winter is best. Further south the Thames can provide good roach fishing in certain areas, but the chub seem to be moving into the ecological niche vacated by the roach.

The Severn has seen a remarkable revival in the fortunes of the roach, but they have not yet returned to every stretch. Roach fishing on the Trent is improving every winter.

Often the largest roach reported today are caught from stillwaters, often by anglers after other species. That is how Nottingham's Richard Jones took his new record fish of 4lb 1oz from a local gravel pit. He was after tench at the time. Deep gravel pits abound in this country, and it is to those that anglers must now look to contact the biggest specimens.

When to fish

The finest river roach fishing is always found in the winter when the fish group up in large shoals, often over clean beds of gravel. Find a smooth glide shallowing up between rush beds and the roach will not be far away.

In summer roach are often out of condition, and difficult to catch. Try oxygenated water such as weir-pools, fishing close to the sill. In lakes you will need to fish early morning or late evening with a slow-falling bait such as bread.

Baits

The last few years have seen one bait revolutionise roach fishing. This is the caster—the sinking chrysalid stage of the maggot. Before that, anglers used chrysalids on the hook, but were unable to groundbait with them as they simply floated away.

The experiments by Benny Ashurst and other North-west matchmen discovered that by either fridging chrysalids, or immersing them in water, shortly after the maggot turned, their development was suspended further. At this stage they sank to the bottom, attracting all species particularly roach. Their big advantage over maggots was they did not crawl away. Maggots are still the most widely used bait for roach, due to easy availability and because of the quick response they bring from fish. But maggots are not selective and can easily attract other small, unwanted species.

For roach, bronze maggots usually work best. One bait that can attract roach quickly is hempseed, boiled until the white shoot is showing. But it is difficult to use on the hook owing to the ultra-fast bites it produces. Matchmen groundbait with hemp to draw the roach, and then fish with casters on the hook. Other seed baits effective in the late summer and early autumn are wheat, tares, and pearl barley.

Bread in all its many forms also works well for roach, especially in the summer. A small hook just covered with a piece of sliced bread from a bread punch will often outfish any other baits on canals, shallow lakes or slow-moving rivers.

The angler interested in the larger specimens can cover a size 10 hook with a fresh piece of bread flake or crust. Legered in a reservoir, gravel pit or fast-flowing river such as the Hampshire Avon, this size bait can attract a two-pounder. In winter when the rivers are bank-high, the traditional tail of a lobworm will produce good fish when legered in slack water.

Bream

The bream is the number one fish to the matchman; and second in popularity only to the roach to the general pleasure angler.

If you seek excitement, reel-screeching runs and powerful dives, then the bream is certainly not for you. However, not everybody has the same opinion of how a fish should play and despite the lack of rushing fight, you still have to take great care while playing a bream—especially a big one.

The fish's attraction is due to its wide-spread population all over the country, and the fact that, as a fish living in large shoals, big catches can be made when you find them.

Techniques

Bream can be caught by a variety of methods, but the best known and most widely practised is the swingtip.

This is simple legering—but with the added sensitivity of a bite indicator, known as a swingtip, fixed on the rod tip. This is a short length of material, usually plastic, much thinner and more sensitive than the actual rod tip, and hinged roughly at right angles.

If sarkandas reed is used, then the hinge is made of rubber tube. The device is fixed to the rod tip by means of a screw attachment.

After casting, your rod is usually placed into two rod rests so that it lies roughly parallel with the bank. Reel in a little line to take up the slack; and the tip should then be pointing as near to straight down as possible.

A small lead like the Arlesey bomb—size depending on conditions, as long as you can hold bottom—is the weight used. Hook size depends on the type of bait. When a fish takes, it will normally swing up and out, signalling a firm bite.

On running water, a quivertip works best. This is made of solid fibreglass, rubbed down to act like a fine rod tip. A straight detector, fixed in the same way as the swingtip, it bends round with a pull of the current.

Bream can also be taken on the float, fished at long range. An antenna fixed bottom ring only can be cast a good distance. Look out for bites on the drop as the bait falls through the water. The float will fail to settle as a fish takes.

When the wind is behind you, try the zoomer float. Made of cane and balsa, this is a long-casting float which incorporates weight. Fish it top and bottom, and look out for lift bites when the float rises, rather than dips, in the water.

When to fish

Bream can be taken all the year round, but there are certain times of the year when big hauls are possible. At the start of the season in June, bream are still formed into vast shoals on their breeding grounds before they break up into small shoals. With summer low water conditions, this spreading out can be delayed for as much as the first month of the season.

Later on, the fish break up into small shoals and spread out to different areas of a fishery. This usually accompanies extra rain water in rivers, then catches become smaller because the shoals are smaller and far more mobile.

In autumn, when the water starts to colour up the bream 'come on' again, feeding far more freely. Early morning and the evening are the recognised times for bream fishing, but many of the really big recorded bream hauls have been taken during all-night sessions.

Location

Bream can be found almost anywhere in the country in rivers, lakes, canals and pits. The only exceptions are the North of Scotland and much of the north-east of England.

Huge shoals of bream can be found in almost any of the East Anglian rivers, like the Witham, Welland, Nene and Ouse. In the same area is the vast Fenland

system of drains and in this maze of waters bream are numerous. They are also found in large numbers in Somerset waters, such as the Huntspill and King's Sedgemoor Drain.

The Thames has been recorded as one of the most famous bream rivers ever, but you cannot talk about bream without mentioning the Norfolk Broads. Every year thousands of anglers flock to the Broads and their adjacent rivers—the Bure, Ant and Thurne—to make big catches. However, for big bream, the established stillwater fisheries cannot be beaten.

Baits

There are four basic baits that every bream angler uses—maggots, caster, worms and bread in its various forms. In different areas, each of these baits has a strong following, and the nationwide popularity of each seems to occur in cycles.

In one season, maggot may be the popular bream bait, yet everyone will turn to caster or worm the following year. For the hook, the soft gozzer maggot is always in demand, while the tiny squat maggots of the house-fly are used as feed in the groundbait. Small red-worms and brandlings are in favour as hook bait, often fished as a combination bait with a caster.

The real advantage of caster over maggot as feed in the groundbait is that it does not attract those trouble-some pests—small eels. This advantage is echoed in what is probably the most popular bream bait of all—bread.

Bread can be fished in a paste form, as flake pulled from the centre of a fresh loaf, and even the crust can be used successfully. Usually fairly big pieces of bread on a largish hook—for example, size 8—tends to put smaller fish off, leaving the bait for bream to find.

Remember to pinch the bread round the shank of the hook only, otherwise you will mask the point.

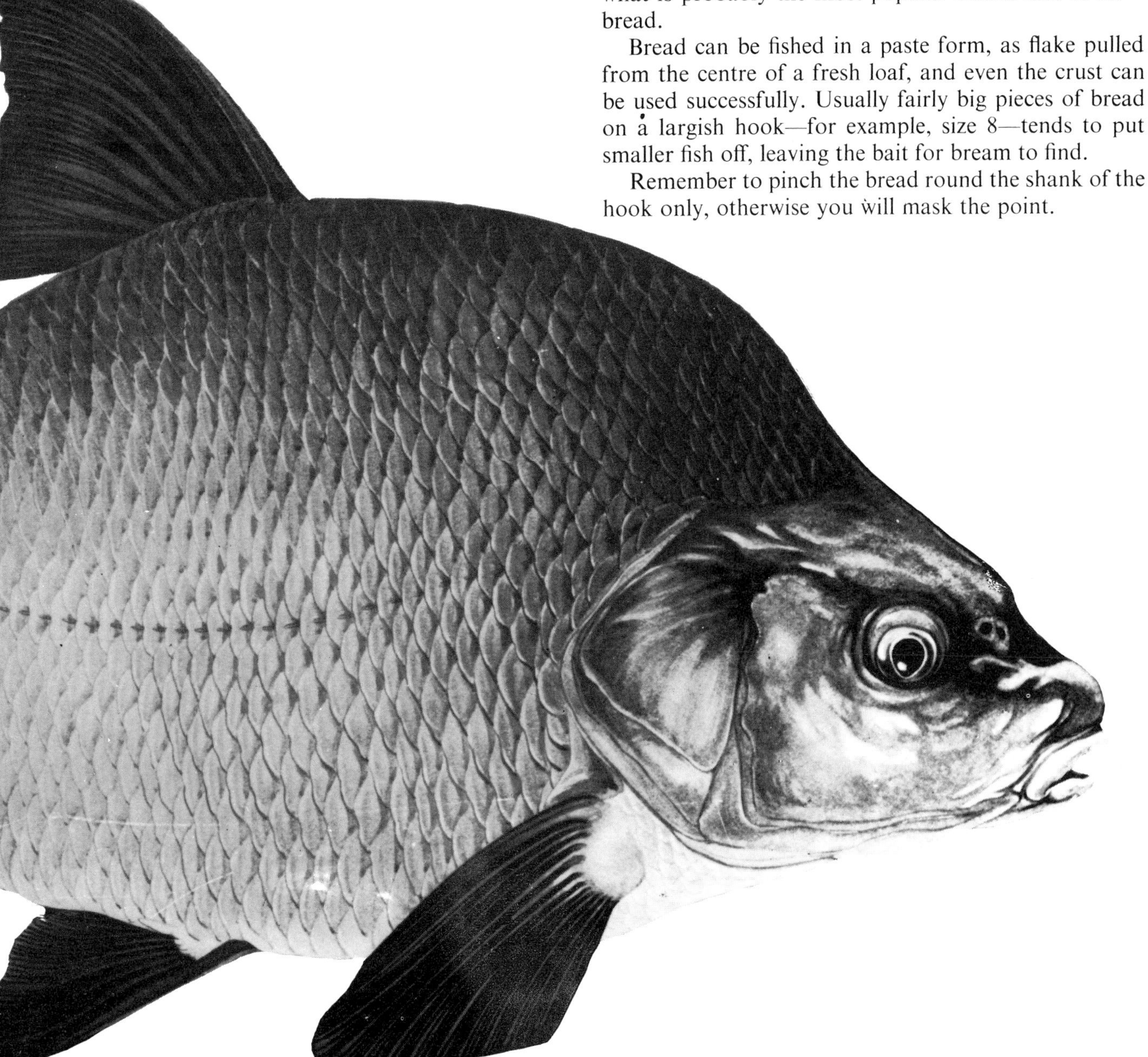

Chub

The chub is one of the shyest of all our river fish but his bite can be the boldest. These paradoxical facts sum up its character.

Techniques

In summer when the water is low and clear, chub can be spotted cruising for food on shallow gravel bars. But suitable cover is never far away—a home where they can bolt at first sign of danger.

Provided you keep well down below the skyline there is no reason why the chub should not take a free-lined bait plopped near it.

In faster, broken water below weirs or fords, chub often congregate in great numbers. Here you will need some weight to keep your bait on the bottom. A small Arlesey bomb will do, but the swan-shot leger works better.

This can be rigged up in seconds, and weight added or subtracted as you need. It holds bottom better by spreading the weight over a greater area. Do not be frightened to fish right among the streamer weed and hold your rod while you feel for bites.

If no chub are showing, choose a swim with a suitable feature. An overhanging willow tree on the far bank or a thick bed of rushes are usually home to a shoal of chub. You will need to cast accurately to put your bait right among them.

As evening approaches, the chub start to move on the surface in search of food. It is now that the fly fisherman can take his fish using a thick bushy dressing like the Palmer. Chub feed right on into the dark, and cheese legered at night can be the deadliest method of all.

While summer chub fishing is often a matter of stalking individual fish, winter chubbing can be even more exciting. Now the fish are having to search more for food, and can be drawn out from their holes by feeding the stream.

Use an Avon-style float and a largish hook baited with maggots, casters or bread. A centre-pin reel can add to the excitement, when you hook a strong fish in a powerful current.

Make sure you turn your fish before it heads for the nearest tree roots. Chub have a cunning ability to transfer your hook from their mouth to the nearest snag.

The chub is not frightened of strong tackle and a 5lb line to a size 4 hook is standard tackle for snaggy swims and that big mouth. But the matchmen take their fair share of chub, too, fishing with much lighter float gear.

The answer is that the chub will pull as much as you pull. Hit it hard with a Mk IV Avon rod and the fish will pull the tip into an arc.

Instead gently set a size 18 hook, on light tackles, into the top lip and play it quietly. Then you can guide the chub into the landing net with the minimum of fuss.

When to fish

A warm evening in late summer can often produce the largest chub of all. The quiet angler watching his rod top as the light fades will be amazed at the power of the fish that bangs his tip down. If he strikes in time, he will enjoy the fight of a lifetime.

Chub certainly feed into the dark during summer, and a swim that seemed dead during the day can come alive at night as the chub go on the prowl.

Winter chub are often the best conditioned fish, firm and fat from fighting the current. Then they move out of the weir and sluice pools into the quieter runs of water, but you can still catch them when ice is freezing the margins.

Location

The cheeky chub has pushed its way into our finest game rivers, challenging the salmon and the trout for supremacy. Herefordshire's River Wye—the home of 40lb salmon—is roamed by giant shoals of big chub, while its neighbour, the Severn, is rated by many as our finest chub river.

Chub love fast water, and the faster the river the bigger its chub. The Hampshire Avon, especially at the Christchurch end, has produced its fair share of seven-pounders, and the Dorset Stour is another renowned chub preserve. The east coast rivers all contain chub in their upper reaches. Norfolk's Wensum and Waveney are now prolific chub waters.

Find a weir pool and you will find a chub. This is why the Thames and its tributaries have such a population of big fish . . . chub that could even break the record. The chub population of the sluggish River Nene is on the increase, especially in its faster reaches, while the upper River Welland is one of England's best rivers for big fish.

Further north, Yorkshire's Ouse and Swale systems regularly produce a crop of specimens, while the species has now got a strong foothold in the matchmen's River Trent. But the most idyllic chub water of all must be the Great Ouse running from the heart of England to empty into the Wash. Chub abound from the six-pounders of Dick Walker's narrow reed-fringed up-stream beat to the shoal fish of the St Ives meadows. A host of mills, sluices and weirs create a wealth of swims for one of our most obliging fish.

Baits

The chub is the most omnivorous of fish devouring everything with equal relish. Anything small that swims, crawls or flies goes down that pink maw.

Of the natural baits, the humble lobworm probably has the most attraction. If you cannot find any worms, try a slug, or even a grasshopper or snail. They will all take chub. Maggots are another chub appetiser, but the caster has more attraction for the larger specimens. You will need to feed plenty in to make them interested.

The most useful chub bait of all is a piece of English cheddar. Cheese must have accounted for more big chub than any other bait. Today there is another trend towards luncheon meat, which seems to work equally well.

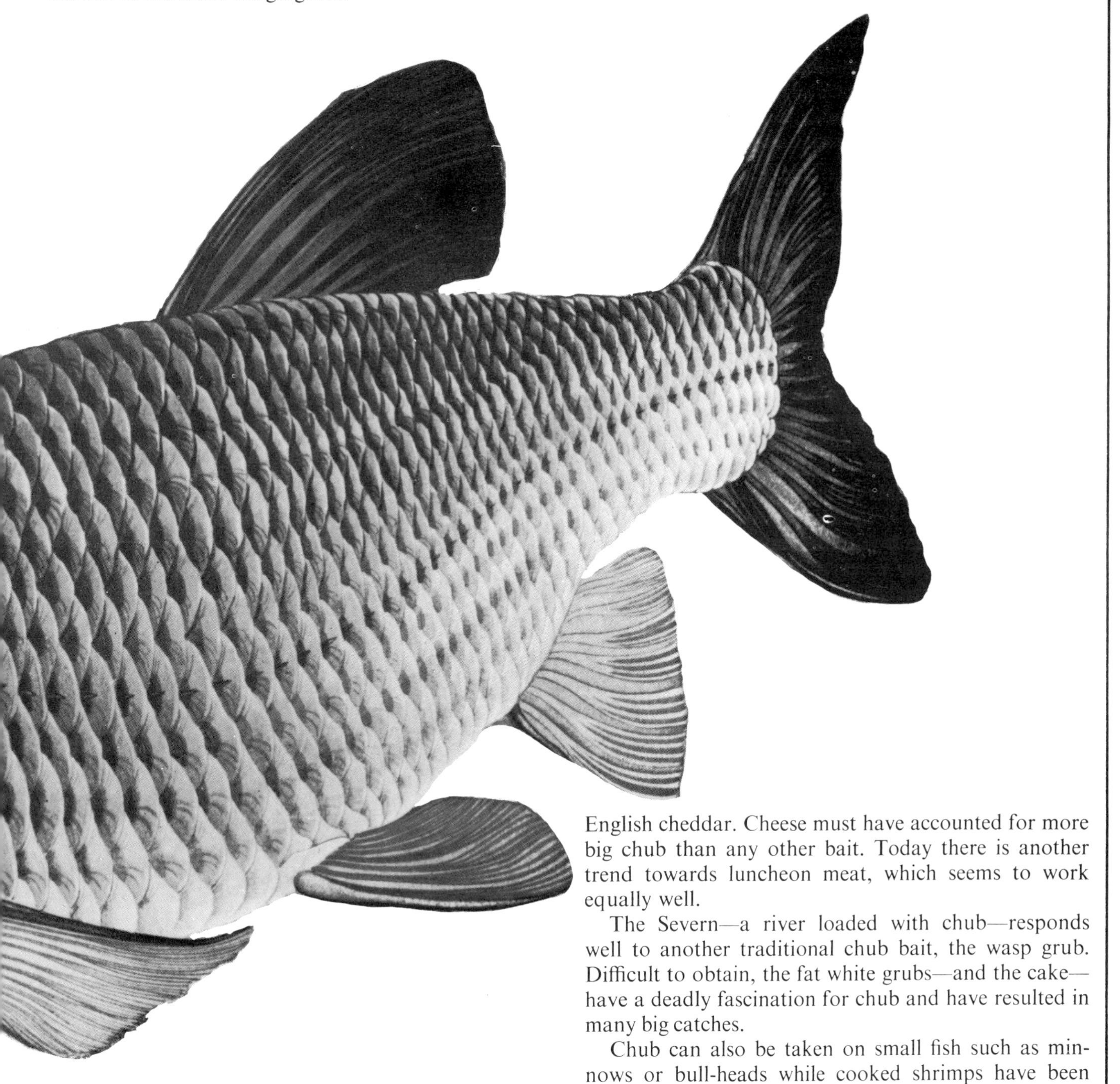

The Severn—a river loaded with chub—responds well to another traditional chub bait, the wasp grub. Difficult to obtain, the fat white grubs—and the cake—have a deadly fascination for chub and have resulted in many big catches.

Chub can also be taken on small fish such as minnows or bull-heads while cooked shrimps have been known to work. You can try a small spinner for the bigger fish, or look for a crayfish—one of the best big-fish baits of all.

Perch

The perch is possibly the most strikingly beautiful fish in Britain. Most people's experience of the perch will be as a small fish—often the first species an angler catches. But as it grows, the perch takes on a charm other fish could never have.

Its high-backed, chunky body is covered with glowing scales varying from a deep, bronzy green on the back, through lighter green flanks, a white belly and crimson fins.

The whole effect, particularly its 'sergeants' stripes, gives the impression of a painting. Combined with a fierce, aggressive-looking head, this makes the perch a worthy-looking opponent.

Techniques

Most perch are caught on float tackle—whether the bait is a worm, grub or small livebait.

Often, sliding floats are used to present the bait in the deep holes perch are so fond of—though a leger rig is the only way to reach them at long range in a lake or gravel pit.

Spinning, fly fishing and small deadbaits all produce perch, but one of the deadliest methods is a freelined minnow or worm. For all these methods, a long, soft-action rod is essential with a fixed spool reel and light line.

Hook sizes vary a great deal, depending on your bait and rig. Sizes 16 for maggots, 14 and 12 for grubs and small worms, and size 6 or 8 for lobworms or livebaits.

A single hook through the upper lip is all you need for a livebait, which can then be fished either with a leger outfit or under a slim-bodied float.

Remember, perch do not have mouths as big as pike, they do not always take a bait as completely and quickly as the latter. Ignore the initial bobbings and strike as the perch runs off with the livebait.

Static deadbaits do not produce many runs from perch—but fish them sink and draw, letting the bait fall to the bottom, reeling it up for a few feet, and then repeating the action.

The wide variety of spinners, plugs, and other lures available all take perch—with fish often taking lures almost as big as themselves. Unlike the solid take of a pike, the perch will often follow the bait, tapping it several times—sometimes without actually taking it. They can often be induced to take by a sudden variation in the speed of retrieve. The top bait for perch has always been the lobworm.

Use a sliding float to reach fish in those deep holes in autumn, or a leger paternoster in really deep or weedy water.

Other fish in the shoal often follow a hooked fish—even to the bank or boat. This is where the fly fisherman can have a real tussle on his hands if he is fishing more than one fly. Often a perch will swim around, dragging other flies around behind him. Other fish in the shoal grab the lures and before you know it, you are playing two or even three fish. Great fun if the perch are small, but very worrying if you happen to contact big fish.

Remember, perch often patrol regular routes in their search for food. Unless they are holed up for the winter, you may find that where you caught fish today will not produce a bite tomorrow. But experience and a working knowledge of these routes will greatly improve your catches.

When to fish

The perch is probably the first fish that most anglers catch. They are a gregarious fish, living in large groups that gradually diminish as they grow older and lose members—until just one or two really big fish remain.

To catch a lot of perch—especially big ones—autumn is the time to go fishing. For it is then that the shoals move into what every angler knows as 'perchy' holes—deep holes in the river or lake bed; swims in the elbow of a bend in a river; and around any bridge, lock or jetty super-structure in the water.

In the early part of the season, river perch can be found on their food-hunting 'patrols'. The shoal follows a regular route in their constant search for food.

In summer, this route will take them through the shallower water, in the runs between weeds, and in shallow, easy flowing water just off the main current.

Location

You will find the perch almost everywhere in this country. A true native of Britain, it enjoys all types of water.

The smallest farm pond or tiny stream right up to the vast lakes and major rivers—they all hold their share of this aggressive little predator.

One of its favourite haunts are the many gravel pits dotted around the country, where they thrive at great depths.

Perch were one of the most abundant species in British waters right up to a period in the late 1960s when vast stocks of the popular fish seemed to disappear almost overnight.

A mystery disease was blamed, but even the top experts could not pinpoint the actual cause. As the majority of dead perch sink to the bottom, no-one can estimate just how many died.

Then there followed a long period when perch catches were a rarity, except for isolated waters that managed to escape the ravages of disease. Thankfully, in recent years more and more perch have been turning up—including some very big specimens.

Perch abound everywhere from Scotland, down through the Lake District, Yorkshire waters, the Midlands, East Anglia and a multitude of southern and West Country waters.

They even abound in exclusive game fishing areas in Wales and Scotland—where other coarse fish have not been able to gain any recognisable foothold.

Probably the most famous areas are the great Cheshire Meres, the Norfolk Broads, and some of the big London reservoirs.

Baits

The perch is basically a predator, but a wide variety of baits will tempt it. Everything from a maggot to an artificial fly will catch perch—though worm and the spinner are the best known methods.

Equally deadly is a small livebait—minnows, gudgeon, stone loach and even small roach, rudd and other perch. The most common way to fish these livebaits is with a single hook through the lip, presented on float tackle.

The favoured method for that ultimate perch bait, the lobworm, is a paternoster leger rig. Other tempters can include any of the 'normal' baits like maggot, or unusual offerings like slugs and grubs.

They have even been known to attack spinners or livebaits of their own size, so do not worry about keeping your offering small. They will more than likely swallow the hook if you do.

Almost any artificial lure is deadly, especially fished 'sink and draw'. One of the most pleasant ways of fishing for perch must be with fly tackle. A floating line and a big, bright sea trout or reservoir lure will take many perch. In fact it is common for anglers using a team of two or three flies to catch several perch at once.

Pike

The pike is the largest of Britain's coarse fish and one of the most sporting. Twenty years ago pike fishing was a crude affair which gave the fish little chance to display its sporting qualities. Today, thanks mainly to the efforts of an ever-growing band of pike fishermen, the pike has become the working man's salmon. Tackle and techniques have been developed and improved, and there is a growing awareness of the need for conservation of pike stocks. A 10 pound pike can put up a tremendous fight and for many anglers a 20-pounder is a fish of a lifetime.

Techniques

The pike is aggressive, but lazy. It prefers to lie in a particular spot, hidden by its natural camouflage waiting for an unsuspecting fish to swim too near. It is these spots that you have to look for. It may be a sheltered hole under an over-hanging tree, a hidey-hole among the weeds, or near a sunken tree.

For a livebait, a single treble hook through the bait's lip is all you need. For larger livebaits, an extra treble can be added for extra holding and hooking power.

A wire trace is a necessity, as a pike's teeth would make short work of nylon. The most popular hooking rig is the two-hook Jardine snap tackle, but for multi-hook dead-bait rigs make your own.

Timing the strike can be difficult. Leave it too long and the hooks may be swallowed; strike too soon and you could miss the fish. A pike picks up a bait and runs anything from a few feet to many yards. Your float will either sink or travel across the surface against the current or wind.

Do not strike this first run. Instead, wait for the fish to stop and turn the bait. Now your hooks will be inside its jaws. When the second run starts, tighten up until you feel the fish. Then strike with a long, steady pull. If you use a multi-hook rig, you can strike on the first run.

There can be no mistaking a take with lure fishing. The fish slams into the spinner or plug with great speed and ferocity, often tugging the rod tip towards the water. The fight of a pike can vary from water to water and even fish to fish. Some put up dogged, pulling battles close to the bottom, while others put up an aerobatic display that would put a rainbow trout to shame. You will need a lively 10-foot carp-type rod.

Never rush a pike. Play it carefully, and watch those teeth as you unhook it before slipping it back safely into the water. A gag and artery forceps are useful here.

When to fish

The traditional time for pike fishing was after the first frosts, but the modern pike hunter seeks his quarry from the end of summer. When the lilies and weed start to die down leaving less cover for the fry, he goes into action with a variety of plugs and spinners.

By autumn livebaiting comes into its own, first light often being the most successful time to bring a run from a heavy fish.

When winter arrives and the water temperature drops, a static deadbait is often the most killing method of all. Now the pike is moving less and will not be keen to chase its prey. A pike may go several days without feeding before it needs to hunt again.

As the cold weather gives way to the first signs of spring the pike has breeding on its mind. The last two weeks of the season—'the back end'—provide the best pike fishing of all. Then the pike feed greedily on the shoaled-up roach and dace before they face the rigours of spawning. A big female pike, fat with eggs, is attended by several smaller males. Locate this breeding hot-spot and you could have a catch of a lifetime.

The fame of the Scottish lochs is internationally known. Loch Ken, in Dumfriesshire, and Loch Lomond regularly produce 20-pounders. Irish loughs have an even better reputation topped by a 53-pounder from Lough Conn in 1920.

In the south, the Hampshire Avon and Dorset Stour probably hold the biggest pike, not forgetting the London reservoirs. Some of the most productive stillwaters are now the new gravel pits dotted all over the country.

Location

Pike are found almost everywhere . . . even in Wales and the West Country where the salmon and trout fraternity have prevented the pike gaining a strong foothold. Rivers, pits, lakes and even small ponds all hold their head of pike—but the best area is Fenland.

Here, hundreds of miles of drains and rivers are host to packs of this toothy predator. The Fen drains hold vast shoals of bream—which in turn maintain a huge pike population.

The Norfolk Broads, once the top spot for pike hunters, have sadly passed their peak. The tragic outbreak of the killer algae prymnesium in 1969 wiped out some of the finest pike fishing in Britain in a matter of weeks—though good fish are showing up again, particularly in the River Bure.

Baits

Pike will eat a surprising variety of baits. Everything from a tiny worm or maggot up to livebaits weighing as much as 6lb or more has produced pike—and they even eat each other.

Waterfowl, frogs, mice, rats and voles have all been known to be included in the pike's diet. But for the angler, there are more conventional baits to use.

Livebait usually means small fish like roach, dace, chub and gudgeon are used. Some pike anglers, however, use bigger baits—up to several pounds or more—in search for bigger specimens.

Deadbaits can include sea fish. The easily-obtained herring, mackerel or sprat are probably the most popular. But there is a current vogue for sardines. These can be fished whole, or in half—using either head or tail.

As far as lure fishing is concerned there is an almost endless variety—spinners, wobblers, vibrating lures, floating and sinking plugs. Deadbaits may be mounted on spinning vanes and worked across the bottom.

All these baits and lures have their place in pike fishing, depending on the water, time of year and conditions. Sometimes a tiny bleak will produce a 20-pounder; other times you may need a 2lb chub.

Sea fishing

Sea fishing is the fastest growing branch of angling. The increased mobility of anglers during the last decade has meant that it is no longer confined to those living near the sea.

It offers not only sport to the enthusiast but also the chance to eat what he catches . . . an increasingly important consideration with high fish prices!

Sea fishing from beach or pier can be relatively inexpensive. Bait can be dug or collected from the sea shore before a fishing session and even old nuts and bolts can be used in place of expensive leads.

Boat fishing is more expensive unless the angler is one of the growing number who now own their own small dinghies. It is often the boat trips which provide the sea angler with his best catches.

Techniques and tackle have improved dramatically in the last twenty years and many anglers are now scaling down their line strengths to allow their quarry a chance to display its fighting qualities.

The distribution of fish along our coastline gives the sea angler a chance to fish for a variety of species during the year. In the summer months he can fish for tope or shark, bass or wrasse. During the winter months he can try his hand at the vast shoals of cod and whiting which come close inshore with the first gales and frosts.

Sea fishing can be a solitary sport or a gregarious one, but the newcomer to sea angling can be certain of one thing—hundreds of miles of free fishing from which to choose.

Basic tackle

Sea fishing splits itself into two categories; boat and beach or pier fishing. Although anglers may fish for the same species the two categories call for totally different tackle and techniques.

It is often best, and a great deal cheaper, to start by learning how to beach fish, graduating to boat fishing when you have mastered the various techniques.

Local knowledge for beach fishing is essential. Most beaches fish best at certain times of the year, some on a rising or flood tide, others on a receding or ebb tide. If you live by the sea you will soon discover this essential information. If you live inland and have to travel, make a point of talking to a regular angler or local tackle dealers. They can be a mine of useful information.

Beach tackle

Rods A long rod is necessary for beach fishing. This enables long casting and keeps your line clear of the waves. A line left low in the water will quickly pick up floating seaweed or become covered with sand or shingle.

Rods made of hollow glass are best; select a rod between 11 and 13 feet depending on your height and build. Beach rods are made to cast specific weights. For general purposes choose one that will comfortably cast four to six ounces. There is little point in buying a rod which is too heavy. You will be unable to get maximum casting power from it. In many beach fishing situations you may have to cast up to 80 yards to find the feeding fish. This makes selecting a rod to match your height and physical frame very important.

Reels For beach fishing choose either a fixed spool reel or a multiplier. The multiplier will cast the furthest distance but is more difficult to master. There are many different sizes and makes on the market, so make sure when buying to tell the tackle dealer the kind of rod it is for. In this way you can build up a properly balanced outfit. For general beach fishing a multiplier should be big enough to take around 200 yards of 20lb line.

The multiplier has a revolving spool encased in a metal cage. At one end of the reel is the handle which is

A long rod is essential for beach fishing as it enables long casting and keeps the line clear of the waves.

A multiplier reel will cast further than a fixed spool reel but is more difficult to master.

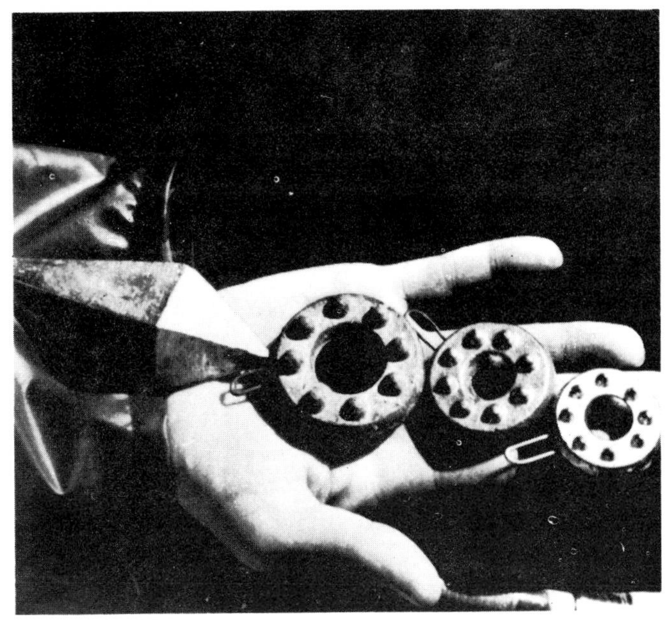

Buy plenty of leads as beach fishing conditions can vary enormously, depending on wind and height of tide.

attached to a series of gear wheels, which in turn are connected to the spool. When casting the handle and gears can be disengaged by a special lever, leaving the line free to run as the cast is made. If left unchecked the spool will turn too fast and the line will tangle. This can be stopped by applying gentle thumb pressure to the spool.

The fixed spool reel is simpler to use but in the smaller models casting distance is strictly limited. As a beginner's reel it is ideal and some makes on the market are beginning to threaten the multiplier's casting supremacy.

Lines Nylon lines are best suited to beach fishing, ranging from 5–6lb for mullet fishing up to 30lb for heavy shore fishing. Buy well-known brands and avoid cut-price ones—their quality can prove doubtful. For most fishing a 15–18lb line is ideal.

Leads Beach fishing conditions can vary enormously, depending on wind and height of tide. Buy plenty of leads ranging from 2–6oz and make sure that most are torpedo shaped with wire legs. These will grip the bottom in strong tides.

Hooks For light beach fishing for flatfish you can buy eyed freshwater hooks from size 6 to the larger size 1. For other types of fishing buy a selection of 1/0; 2/0 and 3/0 hooks.

Traces For beach fishing there is no need to bother with wire traces. Buy some lengths of nylon in varying breaking strains, a selection of swivels and a couple dozen beads of varying sizes and you will have the materials to make up any kind of trace you may need.

Accessories For most beach fishing a good rod rest is essential because beach rods are too heavy to hold for any length of time. A rest can be bought from a tackle shop, or a tripod can be made from three lengths of bamboo cane. Most fish can be safely landed by beach-

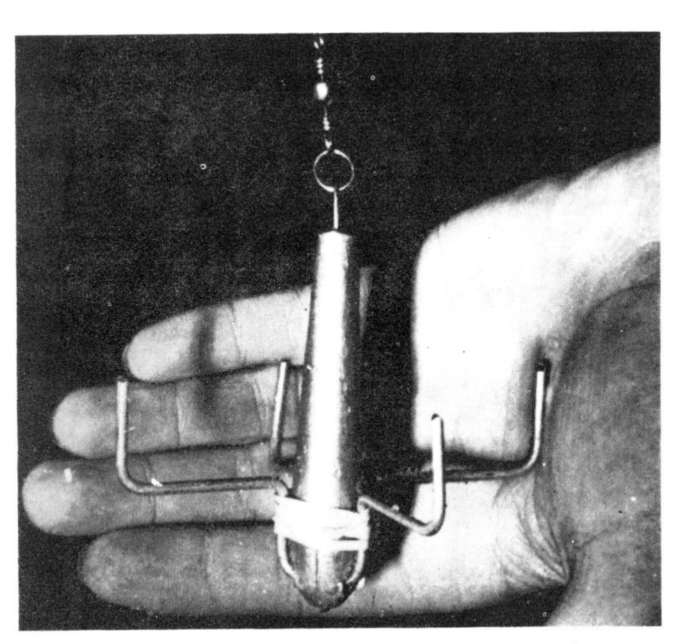

A torpedo-shaped grip lead with wire legs will grip the bottom in strong tides. There are many different types of this lead available.

ing them in shallow water and lifting them by the gills, but for some species a gaff may be necessary. For pier fishing where the angler may be some distance above the water, a dropnet is essential. It can be made from nylon netting, a firm steel frame and some stout rope.

Do not forget to take a sharp knife with you for cutting up bait and a small canvas bag for carrying odds and ends.

Boat fishing

In comparison with beach fishing, boat fishing is far easier but more expensive. Little casting is involved and

A sturdy box, divided into compartments, will help the angler keep his equipment dry and accessible.

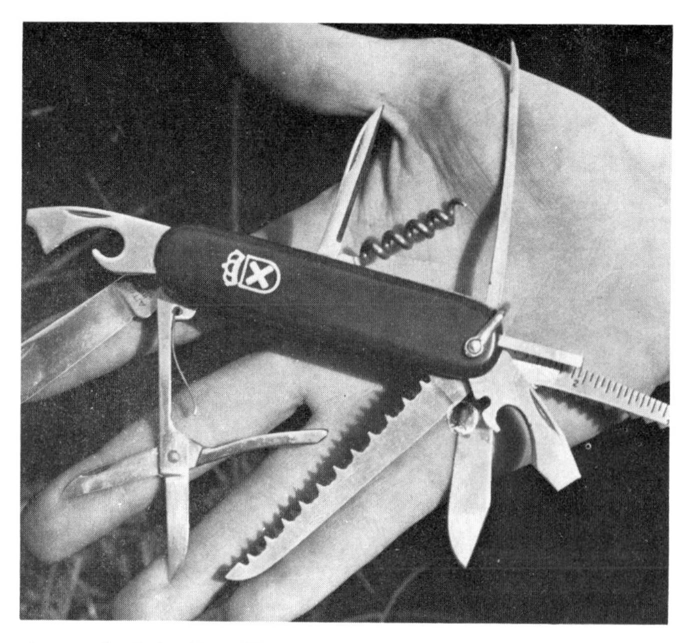

An angler's knife will prove an invaluable piece of equipment for cutting up pieces of bait.

provided you select a good skipper, sport can be fast and furious. An experienced skipper will be able to put his anglers over the best marks; advise them of the species they are likely to catch and the best baits to use.

Rods There is no need for long rods. They should be short—between six and seven feet is ideal. It is a mistake to buy a heavy stiff rod; choose one on the light side and with an action that will allow the fish to display their sporting qualities.

Reels Avoid fixed spool reels when boat fishing. A large multiplier or centre pin reel is ideal. Whichever you choose make sure it will hold at least 200 yards of 35lb nylon or braided line. The heavier weight is necessary because the fish you encounter while boat fishing can be much larger than those taken from the beach.

Lines Lines of 30lb plus are often needed for boat fishing. They can either be nylon or braided synthetic lines, of which Dacron and Terylene are the most common. Whichever type you choose, always inspect it regularly for signs of deterioration and always test the last 20 feet or so for weakness before every fishing trip.

Leads A good selection of leads ranging from 4oz to 1$\frac{1}{2}$lb is needed depending on where you intend to fish. They can be either bomb or bell shaped.

Hooks Invest in a selection of hooks ranging from 1/0 to 6/0 for really big fish. Make sure they are sharp and check regularly while fishing to ensure the points have not blunted.

Traces When boat fishing, species such as conger, tope and skate, which have sharp cutting teeth, are often encountered. Traces of heavy nylon or wire are necessary to prevent them biting their way to freedom.

Accessories As with beach fishing you will also need a wide selection of swivels, beads and a sharp knife.

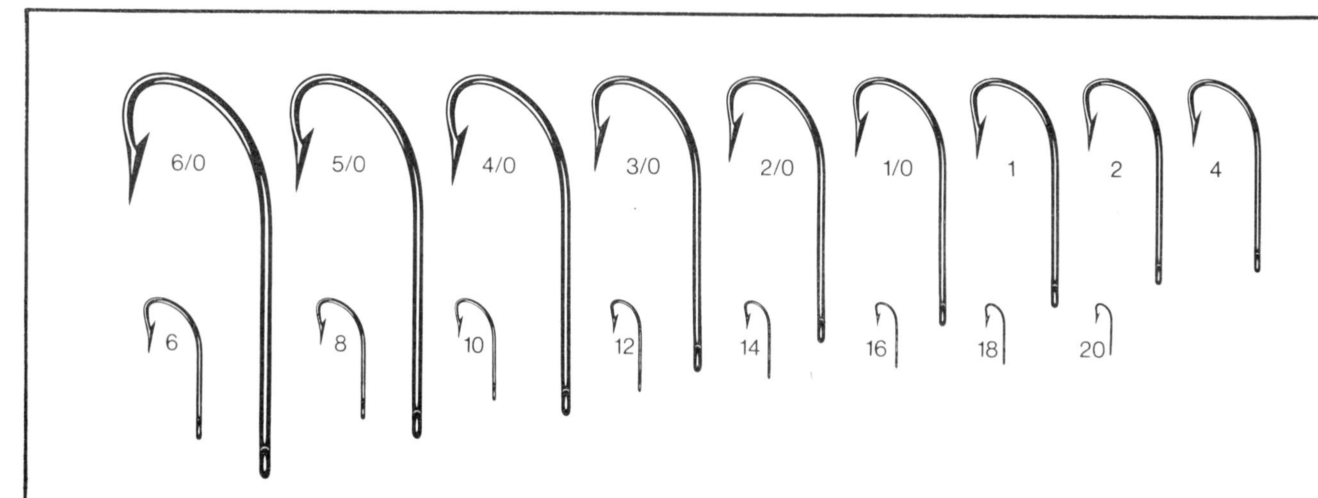

An actual size scale of sea hooks ranging from 6/0 for really big fish, to 1/0 for smaller fish. Sizes 1-20 are freshwater hooks although the larger hooks in this range are often used for small sea fish like plaice and dabs.

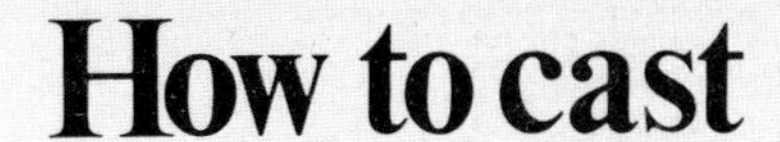

How to cast

Long distance casting is not always a key to success in sea fishing . . . but on many occasions it is the difference between success and failure.

Boat fishing and pier fishing rarely require any great casting proficiency. The beginner, capable only of gently lobbing his bait twenty or thirty yards out to sea, stands just as much chance of putting his bait among the fish as the experienced angler who can cast 100 yards consistently.

However, beach fishing is another matter. On many occasions a 30 yard cast is sufficient—especially on a steep sloping beach or on rocky ground. Usually it is the angler who can cast a 100 yards plus who will catch the most fish.

A suitable beach casting rod, matched to the individual angler so that he is physically capable of making the full use of the rod's power, is essential.

Reels are equally important. The centre pin reel is useless for distance casting and most experienced anglers choose the multiplier. The fixed spool reel, once regarded suitable only for pier, boat and light rock fishing, can also be used to cast long distances. For the beginner it is much easier to master than the multiplier. But the easiest reel for the would-be distance caster to master is the side casting reel—a centre pin reel which works on the fixed spool principle.

Whatever the angler's choice he should take every opportunity to practice his casting. A field, or a piece of open land will give him the opportunity to master his tackle and improve his distance. A great deal of fishing time can be wasted by the angler who has not practised and he may end up spending more time sorting out 'bird's nests' than presenting his bait to hungry fish.

The side caster

Many of the top tournament casters start by using fixed spool reels and then progress to the sidecast reel. The sidecasting reel is one of the easiest of reels to master. Complete beginners can soon cast 100 yards with very little practice. An 18lb line with a 35lb shock leader will handle weights of up to 6oz.

1. *In one flowing movement the lead and rod are swung back for backward compression.*

2. *Stand with your left shoulder facing the sea with the left foot at right angles to the direction of cast. The right foot should point away from the sea. As the lead and rod are swung back weight goes on to the right foot with the knee slightly bent.*

3. *The caster is at the start of the forward movement with his left hand gripping both rod and reel. The thumb stops the line on the edge of the spool. The right hand, which does most of the work, grips the rod at a comfortable distance from the left hand.*

4. *The rod is stretched well behind with right leg bent and weight on the right foot.*

5. *The rod tip is lowered allowing even more weight and body movement in the cast. The arms start to bring the rod round, building up forward compression.*

6. *As the body and arms turn, the right arm lifts the rod with both arms pushing forward. Weight is transferred to the left leg, the right foot twisting forward and right leg straightening.*

7. *The power moment of the cast with rod under full compression. The rod is brought round and up to aim the lead high, with the line on point of release.*

8. *The line has been released and the body turned to face the sea. All weight is on the left foot, the right has twisted forward through 180 degrees.*

The multiplier

Most shore anglers are confirmed multiplier men. Their favourite weapon is often a reel stripped of the level wind mechanism and associated gears. With no brake blocks the reel has a completely free spool allowing casts of 170 yards plus.

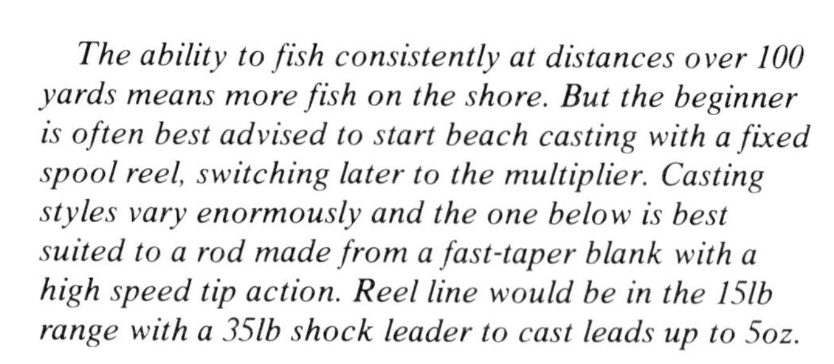

The ability to fish consistently at distances over 100 yards means more fish on the shore. But the beginner is often best advised to start beach casting with a fixed spool reel, switching later to the multiplier. Casting styles vary enormously and the one below is best suited to a rod made from a fast-taper blank with a high speed tip action. Reel line would be in the 15lb range with a 35lb shock leader to cast leads up to 5oz.

1. *Point the rod at 1 o'clock bending the right leg and leaning the body forward with left foot outstretched in the direction of the cast. Swing the lead in a pendulum action just clearing the floor.*

2. *Swing the rod up and back to the 4 o'clock position. The lead swings under the rod reaching a pinnacle high in the air above the tip. The left arm should now be outstretched in front of you.*

3. *With left arm still outstretched pull the rod down and round. At the same time turn the body in the direction of the cast and drop the left foot flat on the floor.*

4. *The power is now built up. Rapidly accelerate the cast as the body turns to compress the rod. Push away with the right foot and transfer body weight to the left. The rod is almost bent double with the applied force.*

5. *The hands will now be level with the chin. The left arm should still be outstretched. Now start to pull down with the left hand and push upwards with the right.*

6. *Now the body is under the rod. The right arm gradually pushing forward, the left pulling towards the body. The lead must always follow the arc of the rod otherwise it can fly off to the right.*

7. *The thumb is released from the reel when the rod is at 55 degrees. The right arm is now fully stretched, the right foot lifting off the floor.*

8. *The left arm is now bent and tucked into the body with rod butt pointing to the middle of the chest. This ensures that a good height is reached. It is important to keep the length of line from rod tip to lead constant. Once you've worked out the most suitable length hold the rod vertically and mark where the lead touches the rod.*

Sea baits

The list of baits that will catch sea fish is endless. Any angler fortunate enough to live by the sea will have a ready-made supply of various baits which he can gather himself before a fishing trip. The inland sea angler is not as lucky. He will have to ensure he has a sufficient supply of bait laid on before setting out for the day.

Lugworms

The lugworm is the most commonly used of all sea fishing baits. It will account for virtually every species of fish that is not exclusively predatory. A marine worm, it is widely distributed and, like maggots for coarse anglers, obtainable from most coastal tackle shops.

It is a relatively simple matter to dig your own lugworms. They can be found on mud and sandy beaches wherever there is some protection from the force of the surf. They are easy to spot as they leave casts of excreted sand. The worm lies on a U-shaped burrow, 12 to 18 inches down. In cold weather, the worms will burrow even deeper. An ordinary garden fork can be used to dig them out, but make sure the prongs are flat, not rectangular.

It is best to dig with a colleague, as it is surprising how many worms can be missed when a forkful of sandy mud is turned over. Quite a few worms will probably be cut by the fork. Unless you intend to fish immediately, throw them away. If you put them with your main supply they will sour, and kill them.

Never put lugworms in tins as they will quickly die. Simply wipe them clean of surplus sand by running them through your fingers and then store them in a plastic or wooden box. Wash the boxes clean in salt water and lay the worms inside them on paper. If you have worms left over at the end of the day and want to keep them for the next day, place the whole ones on sheets of newspaper, so they are not touching each other. Cover them with more newspaper and build up layers. Always store worms in a cool place.

Ragworm

This is a larger and much livelier worm than the lug. It is at its best when used in daylight, especially from the shore. For night fishing the lug, which has a stronger scent, is a much better bait. Although there are many different species of ragworm, there are only three kinds which concern the angler.

The smallest rag, usually just a couple of inches long, can be found in harbour and estuary mud. A forkful of mud will often produce a couple of dozen little worms. A bunch of them will make a good bait for mullet.

The medium sized worms, about five or six inches long, are found on stony, muddy shores near the low tide mark. They have pinchers in their tail which can give a nasty nip, so take care when baiting with them.

The best bait of all are the king rags, worms which are often more than a foot long. Used whole they are a superb bait for really big fish, or they can be cut into pieces. Unfortunately they are not widely distributed. They prefer gravelly mud close to the low tide mark.

Ragworms are best used in daylight, especially from the shore. There are three different species.

Lugworms are used to catch virtually every species of fish that is not exclusively predatory.

Ragworms last longer than lug and should be kept constantly moist.

Crab baits

These make fine baits, especially for bass. Hardback crabs will catch fish, but because of the difficulty of mounting them on the hook the sea angler normally uses soft, or peeler crab. The crab's shell does not grow with the crab; at certain stages the shell is shed revealing a new, but soft shell underneath which hardens after a few days. When the old shell is about to be shed the crab is a 'soft'. During this process the crabs hide in rock pools and under stones. They can be gathered easily and should be kept in a wooden box and covered with seaweed which has been moistened with saltwater.

Having removed the hard shell from the peeler, fish the crab on a single hook. Elastic thread is useful to keep the bait on the hook—just twist it a few times round hookshank and crab.

Fish baits

For anglers unable to obtain a supply of fresh worms or crabs, these baits make an excellent alternative. Mackerel, in particular, is a superb bait for the major species.

In many parts of the country boat anglers can catch their own supply of fresh mackerel on weighted feathered traces. Frozen mackerel are also easily obtainable from most fishmongers. Strips are cut from the fish, the size depending on the type of species likely to be encountered and the bait hooked at the thick end of the strip. Other fish baits which can be used to equal effect are herrings, pilchards and sprats.

Squid

An excellent bait for all kinds of boat fishing and one that is attractive to inshore bass too. Squid can be bought from tackle dealers and stored in a freezer. It can be used whole for really big fish or cut into small strips and fished as a cocktail bait with a couple of lugworms. When using squid remember to use a suitable large hook and one from which the hook point protrudes sufficiently.

Shellfish baits

Mussels and cockles make a useful addition to the sea angler's bait armoury. Prolific along many stretches of coastline, both can be easily gathered by the beach angler, saving a fortune in bait bills. Mussels are widely used in the North-east and Scotland but are largely ignored in other parts of the country. Open them with a knife by inserting the tip into the straight edge of the shell and working upwards, cutting the muscle that holds the shells together.

Insert the hook into the white disc of the flesh, wrap it round the hookshank and then re-insert the hook point in the dark disc.

Cockles make a useful beach bait for flatfish. In areas where they abound they can be scraped from the sand or mud with a rake, or dug out by hand. They can be fished two at a time on a small hook or used as a cocktail bait with lugworm or ragworm.

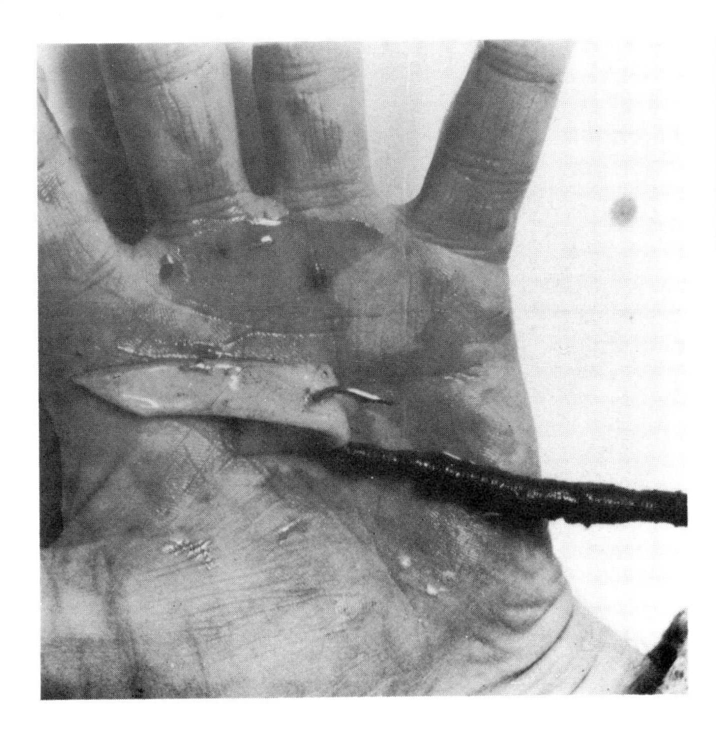

Squid strip and lugworm cocktail.

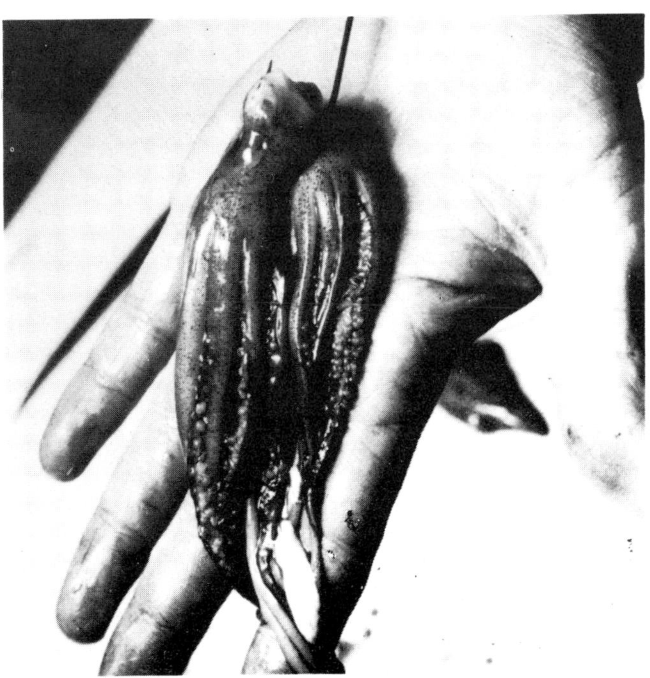

Whole squid—a mouthwatering bait for big cod.

Mackerel baits

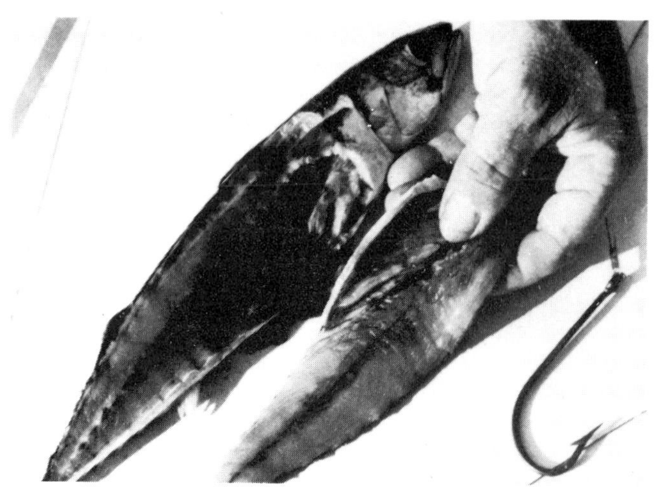

1. *Mackerel baits. Strips are cut from the fish. Their size depends on the type of fish likely to be encountered.*

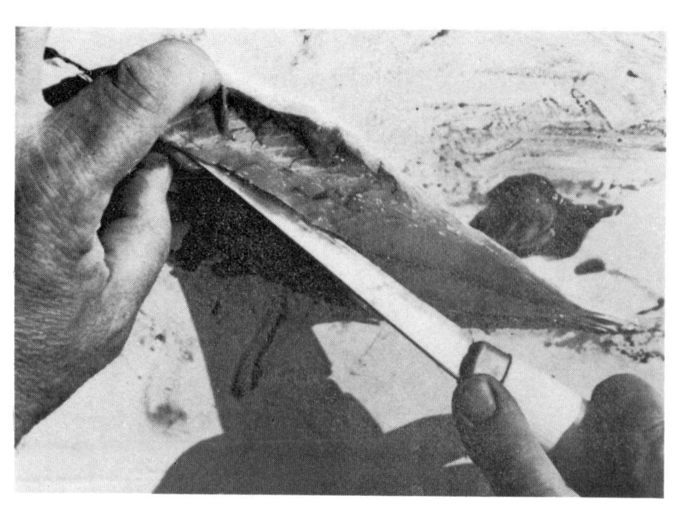

2. *Having taken a fillet from one side of the mackerel cut it in half lengthways.*

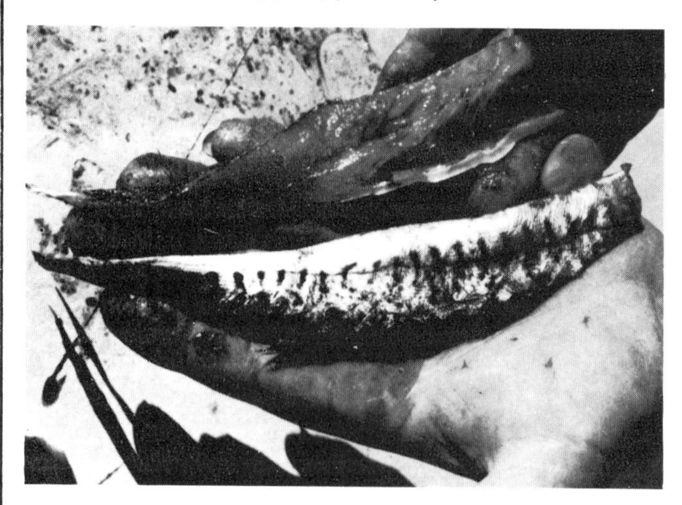

3. *You will now have two strips of mackerel ready to be hooked up.*

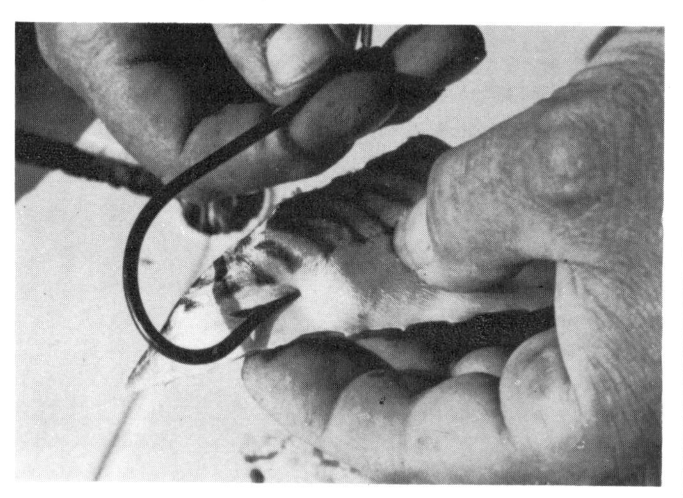

4. *The bait must be hooked at the blunt end of the strip, starting on the skin side.*

5. *When the hook has gone through, twist it and bring back the hook through the fleshy side.*

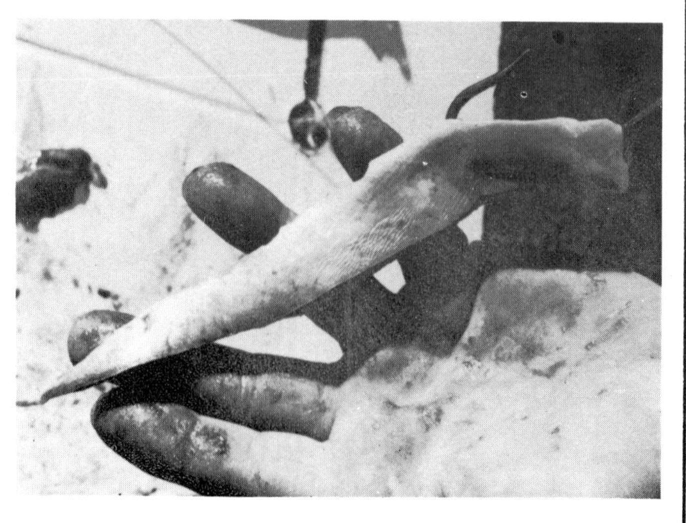

6. *The hook now re-appears on the skin side of the mackerel and the bait is ready for use.*

Digging for lugworms

1. *The tell-tale sign of lugworm in residence—the worm cast (right) and the blow hole. The worm is in a U shaped tunnel between the two holes.*

2, 3. *Digging between the cast and blow hole marks the angler must be quick to grab the worm.*

4. *The worm has been taken intact from its burrow. Damaged worms can be used on the hook but should be kept apart from the rest of the bait.*

5. *The end result, a big black lugworm, a superb bait for most sea fish. He must take care not to damage the worm.*

Hooking lugworms

The hook is the smallest yet most important piece of any sea angler's gear. Yet how many anglers fall into the trap of paying £50 for a decent casting outfit, yet willingly accept a cheap,thick wired hook and bait-up carelessly.

Special sliced-back hooks are available, yet far more effective bait holders can be made quite easily. If cod are the target, a size 2/0 or 3/0 fine-wire Aberdeen is ideal.

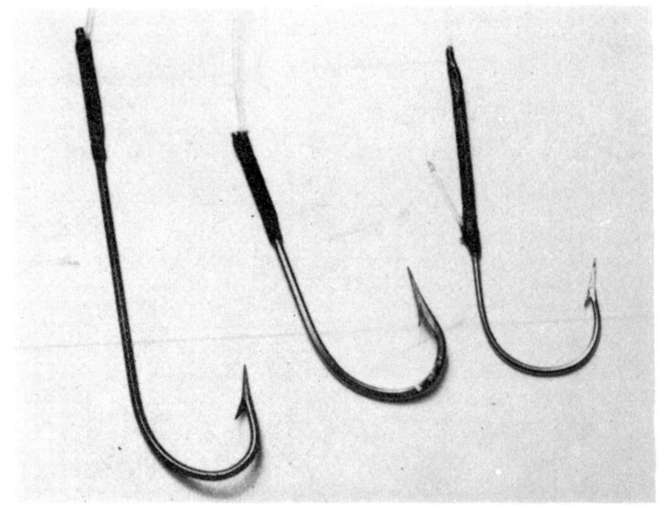

1. *The two hooks on the left are perfect for boat fishing where long casts are unnecessary. The third hook is a modified Aberdeen with short nylon spur.*

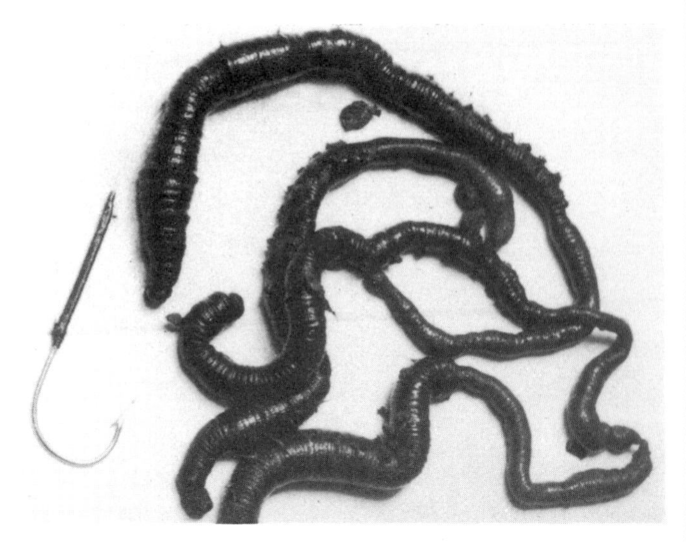

2. *The hook and bait for beach fishing. With care, four or five can be threaded, making a king sized lugworm no cod can resist.*

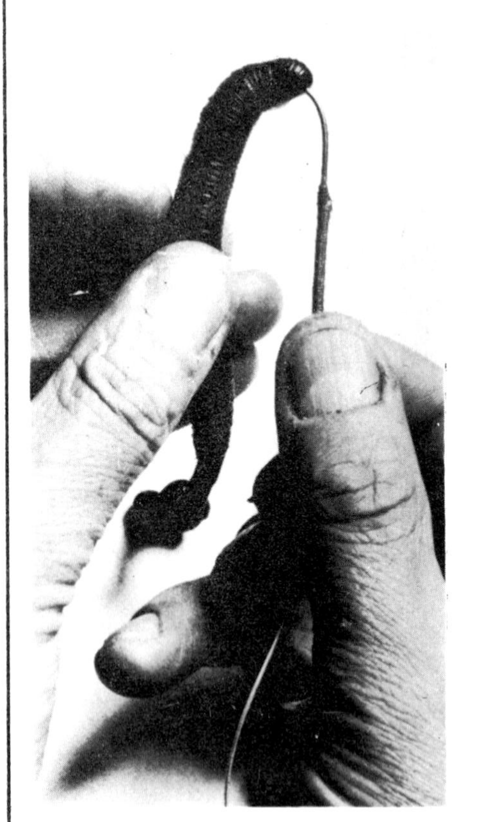

3. *The first worm is slid on to the hook. Great care should be taken not to burst the worm. The smelly juices are most effective on the sea bed.*

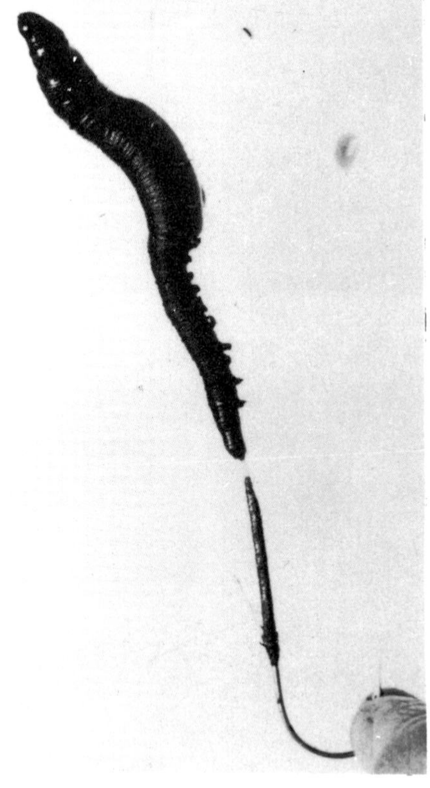

4. *The unbroken worm is pushed up the snood to be followed by the second. The last worm should go on tail first, leaving the big juicy head at the business end.*

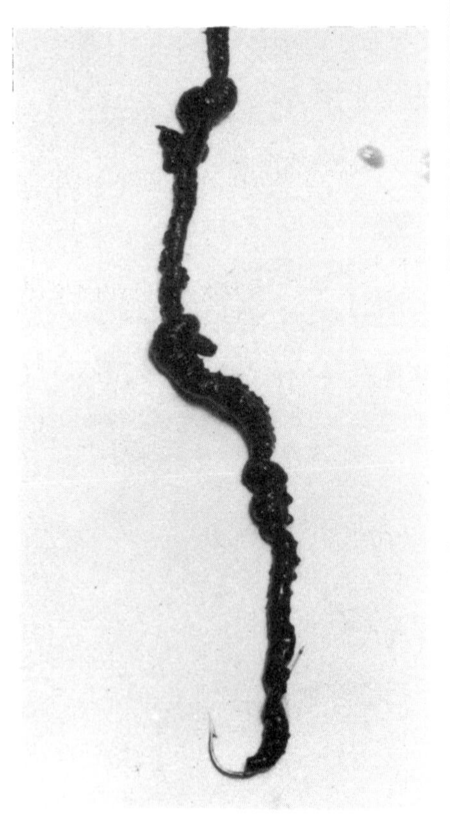

5. *The completed bait, which will not bunch into an ugly bunch of black skins during the cast. The whole bend should be left clear of bait.*

Beach fishing

Beach fishing is by far the most popular branch of sea angling. Britain's coastline offers hundreds of miles of free shore fishing for the angler with the most accessible beaches concentrated along the east coast from the Wash right through to the Kent and Sussex shorelines.

In summer the beach angler can expect a variety of fish. Flatfish, eels, bass and rays can all be taken from the shore. In the winter the picture changes dramatically with cod and whiting becoming the predominant species.

The experienced beach angler will already know the best spots for particular species on his favourite piece of coastline. Just as in all forms of sea fishing, fish gather in particular spots or follow quite definite migratory paths at certain times of the year.

The beginner can gather useful information at low tide, taking note of patches of broken ground, deeper channels and gullies along the coastline he intends to fish.

All these are holding spots at high tide and give the angler a chance of putting his bait where the fish can intercept it.

Long casting is often essential to beach fishing. It may only be necessary to fish 60 yards out to catch fish. But the angler who can cast double the distance will double his chances of catching fish.

Line strength will depend on the species likely to be caught, but there is little need for really heavy lines. A line in the 15–20lb range is often sufficient on sandy beaches—a 25lb line is more suitable for anglers fishing over rocky ground. The greatest stress to line is when the cast is made. Breakages can be kept to a minimum by tying several yards of heavier line, to which the lead and hooks are attached, to the reel line. This 'shock leader' will absorb the added stress of casting and help prevent the end tackle snapping off if a jerky cast is made.

For most forms of beach fishing a breakaway grip lead is the most useful. Tidal currents along our coast tend to run parallel to the shoreline, and the force of these movements will help the wires on the grip lead bite into the sea bed like an anchor to keep the bait hard

A beach angler's paradise—a deserted beach, the swell of surf and the prospect of feeding bass.

on the bottom. When the angler strikes or wants to retrieve his bait the wires on the lead will collapse automatically, leaving him to play a fish or reel in without fear of the wires snagging on an obstruction.

End tackle should be kept as simple as possible. For most forms of beach fishing the basic running leger rig is as effective as any. It makes casting easy by offering little resistance, and is virtually tangle proof.

More complicated, multi-hooked paternoster rigs can be used from the shore, but casting distance will be lost through added resistance and there is more chance of the end rig tangling and failing to offer a natural bait to feeding fish. Casting from a crowded beach when there is a strong tidal pull requires careful thought if tangles with other anglers are to be avoided. The angler who casts straight in front of him will find his tackle swept downtide and inshore before the lead grips. Distance, often a vital factor, will have been lost and his tackle will probably have fouled that of the angler downtide.

The angler who casts uptide will find his tackle will settle in front of him but will also lose casting distance in the process. If there is room on the beach the best method is to walk a few yards uptide, cast, and then return to the original fishing position. The end tackle will settle directly in front of the angler and no casting distance will be lost.

The beach angler's quarry

Winter beach fishing is dominated by whiting and cod with the exception of the West Country shoreline where other species can still be caught. Most of these cod beaches are wide, featureless expanses and local knowledge is often the key to big catches. Night fishing, especially when it coincides with favourable tides, is often the best time for cod and whiting.

Choice of baits is wide but the most productive is undoubtedly the lugworm. Three or four threaded on to a suitable hook provides a tasty morsel for scuttle-mouthed cod.

Small cod—up to five or six pounds—will often signal a bite by a sharp tap on the rod top. They should be struck immediately, with the angler first taking up the slack until he feels the fish and then setting the hook with a steady sweep of the rod. Big cod will usually pull the rod tip down and keep going. Never leave your rod unattended when cod fishing—you may return to find it gone!

The same tactics and bait will also catch whiting although shoals of small fish can be a bait stealing nuisance to the cod angler. Whiting will attack fish strip baits avidly and the angler fishing for them should scale his bait and hook size down accordingly.

Whiting will produce a series of taps on the rod end and striking is a matter of personal judgement.

As the cod and whiting shoals move offshore during March the beach angler is likely to experience the leanest sport of the year.

Flounders, especially in estuaries and estuary mouths, can provide worthwhile entertainment if the angler scales his tackle down to near freshwater standards. However, the main spring species for the beach angler is the thornback ray.

Thornbacks are to be found all round the British coast on clean ground and can be caught all year round. But during April and May there is a general inshore movement of the shoals. They can usually be caught on a wide variety of baits, from worms and soft crabs to fish strips. Whatever bait is used it must be fresh.

Wherever possible, fish for the thornback with as light a line as possible and a basic running leger rig. Wire traces are unnecessary, although a 30lb length of nylon at the business end of the tackle is sometimes needed to counteract the ray's strong grinding teeth. The first arrival of a thornback is often signalled by a bump on the rod tip as the fish flops on the bait.

Summer gives the beach angler the most varied styles of fishing from which to choose. In the South-west he can fish for species like wrasse and conger from the rocks; along the south coast he can fish for mullet, dabs, plaice and even mackerel. But one species stands above all as the most sought after summer and autumn species—the bass. Bass fishing from the shore has attracted a fanatical following among beach anglers, equalled only by the ever-growing band of winter cod enthusiasts.

A typical sight on hundreds of East Anglian beaches during the autumn and winter months. A cod hunting angler flexes his rod on the backswing before powering his bait out to sea.

The side casting reel which has put distances of one hundred yards, often essential in beach fishing, within the reach of every novice.

The multiplier reel, the choice of most beach fishing experts. Although difficult to master this reel, in the hands of an expert, can cast baits 150 yards or more.

Bass are usually found south of a line drawn from Anglesey to the Wash, although a few specimens are caught each year further north. The inshore shoals of bass can be caught from virtually every kind of beach and estuary, covering large areas of sea in their search for food. Shallow water where there is a strong tide run is a favourite haunt, as are surf and storm beaches. Bass can be caught by spinning with a light spinning rod and 10lb line. Distance casting is not always necessary as the fish will often be found in water only a few inches deep.

The largest fish nearly always fall to legered baits with the beach angler aiming to position his bait over any sandy patches when fishing over mixed or broken ground. When fishing broken ground, bomb-shaped leads are best if snags are to be avoided and the lead should always be attached to a 'rotten bottom'—a length of line with a lower breaking strain than the reel line. If the lead becomes snagged the 'rotten bottom' will snap off minimising tackle losses.

A running leger rig should be used if snags are to be avoided. Most beach anglers fish from clean bottomed beaches. Storm beaches, which face the prevailing South-westerlies, are ideal for bass, with the fish following the ebbing or flowing tide in search of food.

Multi-hooked paternoster rigs can be used and long casting is often pointless with the fish coming to within a few yards of the beach. Bass will accept almost any bait but show a marked preference for peeler crab, lugworm and fish baits.

Landing fish

For some types of shore fishing, notably conger and thornbacks, the angler will require a gaff to land his fish. For most other types of beach fishing, large fish can be landed by beaching. When the fish is played out it can be brought into the breakers on a tight line and literally washed ashore by the waves. Some fish are lost by this method when the hookhold tears free, but the beginner will soon master the art. A combination of a sharp hook, properly maintained tackle and firm but gentle pressure will account for most fish.

Never rush a hooked fish, and try not to panic if you hook a really large specimen. Keep calm and let the tackle do the work.

The simple way of landing a fish. By carefully using firm pressure and the action of the waves this angler has drawn a hooked thornback to the water's edge while still maintaining control over the fish.

Boat fishing

During the last fifteen years boat fishing has mushroomed. Higher standards of living and increased mobility have led to a tremendous growth in the number of anglers owning their own small dinghies; and adventurous charter skippers have opened up an exciting new branch of sea angling—wreck fishing.

Dinghy fishing is restricted only by the availability of boat launching sites and beaches. And with most of Britain's east coast ideally suited to small boat launching the Norfolk, South-east and Sussex coastlines have become hotspots for dinghy anglers.

Small boat tactics are largely dictated by the species of fish the angler is trying to catch. The distribution of these species is largely governed by the time of year, although there are always lots of regional variations. March and April are always the poorest times of the year for sea anglers. In most coastal areas the cod have moved offshore and the spring inshore thornback migration has not yet begun. In the summer months the boat angler will have a variety of fish to choose from, including bass, rays and flatfish. As soon as Winter approaches cod and whiting will take over as the predominant species, changing the angler's tatics accordingly.

Summer dinghy fishing offers the angler a variety of choices and tactics. If he fishes from the Essex, Kent and South-east coasts he will encounter bass, flatties, rays and the occasional cod.

The Norfolk coast is less productive in summer with only the tope of the Wash along with rays, a few flatfish, mullet and the odd bass providing any real sport.

There are dozens of regional variations on boat fishing techniques, but there are basic rigs which are not only simple to use but will also lure most species under most conditions.

One of the biggest problems with boat fishing is to overcome the bumping of the lead as it rises and falls with the pitching of the boat. Casting 20 yards away from the boat, instead of just dropping the weight over the side, will help combat this.

Leads whould be carefully chosen so they will anchor the bait firmly to the sea bed without being unnecessarily heavy. A good boat angler should be prepared to change his lead as the tide increases or slackens.

Any running leger rig will soon improve the dinghy angler's catches. The rig may consist of a Kilmore or Clements boom stopped by a bead on the main line, but

The spectacular boom in charter boat wreck fishing has led to hauls of fish like this. Fast, well equipped boats skippered by professional fishermen operating from the Devon and Cornish ports have given many sea anglers an addictive taste for this sport.

it is vital the line should run freely when a fish bites. When fish like cod are really feeding hard in a strong tide tackle resistance may make little difference. But a free-running leger rig will turn finnicky bites into boated fish time and time again.

Never be afraid to experiment with tackle rigs. Switching to a lighter or heavier lead, changing hook size or changing the distance between lead and bait will often produce bites during otherwise blank spells.

Paternoster rigs incorporating the ironmongery of the French boom are best avoided. The angler can just as easily fish two or more hooks at different depths by tying snoods onto his main line, As with all types of angling the old maxim 'keep it simple', is sound advice.

The angler lucky enough to live in an area visited by migratory mackerel shoals can enjoy fabulous sport with light gear. A light spinning or freshwater rod with light line to match will allow the fish to display its tremendous sporting qualities—and give the angler a day's sport to remember. Slightly heavier gear can be used to troll or spin for bass in summer.

The angler will need a gaff or landing net to boat sizable fish safely. Always be careful when attempting to boat large fish—many an angler has disappeared overboard during the excitement. For many kinds of dinghy fishing a large landing net is sufficient but the wise boat angler will also take a gaff. Many species can be landed simply by lifting them by the gills. But if in doubt, use the net or gaff.

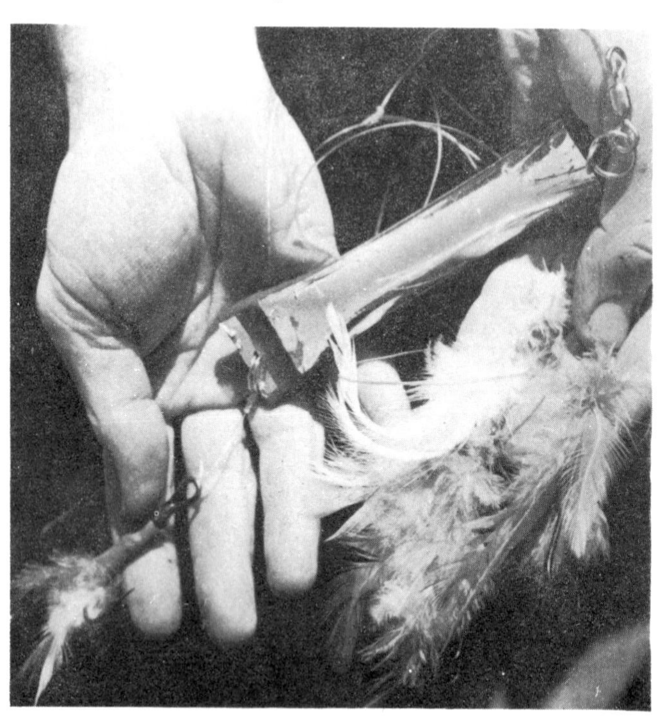

One of the most effective methods of taking big catches of coalfish, pollack, cod and ling from wreck marks has been pirking. The pirk (above) is simply a flashy, heavy, metal lure with hooks attached, worked sink and draw over the wreck. This one has the added attraction of feathers.

Charter boat fishing and wrecking

During the last decade many anglers, especially inshore enthusiasts have turned to the charter boats for their fishing. Every major sea angling centre now has its own fleet of full-time charter boats, catering for groups of individual anglers or club parties. The majority of these skippers are keen anglers themselves and will do their utmost to provide a good day's fishing for their party.

The charter boats are advertised in the angling press and local tackle shops often serve as booking centres. The charge per angler for a day's fishing can vary but some prices do include bait and tackle hire. The beginner is best advised to make his first charter trip with a group of experienced anglers and with a skipper recommended by them. Some skippers allow the angler to keep all the fish he catches; others limit each angler to two fish. If unpleasant arguments are to be avoided over this controversial issue, the angler should check on the skipper's rule when booking a boat.

The charter boat skipper will probably have years of local angling experience and should be able to place his party over a productive mark or at least in an area where fish are likely to be intercepted at some state of the tide. The more expensive charter boats are often equipped with sophisticated fish finding equipment, which guarantees that the angler is fishing right over large shoals of fish.

The most sophisticated boats of all are to be found operating from the South-west ports along the Devon

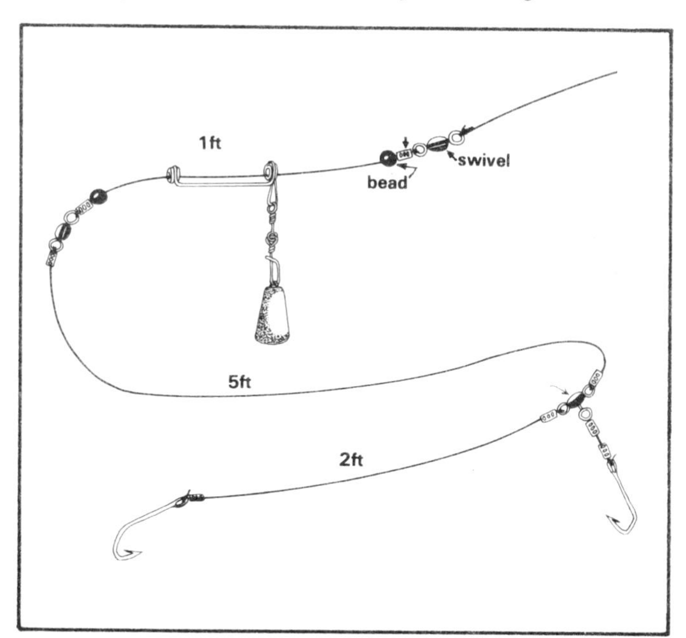

Above: A typical two hook running leger rig for general boat fishing. The lead is attached to the reel line by means of a Clement's boom.

Right: One of the most exciting moments of boat fishing—the gaffing of a large fish. Many a good fish has been lost by poor gaffing—so when in doubt leave it to the professional, the boat skipper.

and Cornwall coasts.

The hundreds of wrecks off this stretch of coast have added a whole new dimension to charter boat fishing. The wrecks provide natural larders and holding spots in these already prolific waters and hugh catches of conger, ling, coalfish, pollack and cod have been taken by boats operating from Plymouth, Brixham and Mevagissey.

Although normal charter boat fishing techniques are often much the same as dinghy fishing tactics, wreck fishing relies heavily on the use of artificial baits.

While fish strip or mackerel fillet baits can be fished on or above the bottom for conger, pollack, ling and coalfish, good sport can be had by using artificial sand-eels or pirks—heavy, shiny chrome lures with trebles attached. As tackle losses over wreck marks can be heavy many anglers make their own pirks, often out of bicycle handlebars.

The artificial lure is lowered over the wreck and worked sink-and-draw fashion until a fish takes. Wreck fishing is an arduous sport, both for angler and tackle. Tackle must be strong to deal with the big fish likely to be encountered and the angler should have some previous experience of charter boat fishing.

No chapter on boat fishing would be complete without a mention of the dangers involved. Every year boat anglers are drowned because they fail to obey the basic safety laws. Would-be dinghy owners should first ensure they have plenty of sea-going experience before buying a boat. Before a fishing trip they should obtain a weather forecast. If the weather is bad or the sea unexpectedly choppy, they should not attempt to put to sea.

Never overcrowd a small dinghy. Boats up to 12 feet overall should not have more than two passengers; those up to 14 feet never more than three.

All dinghy anglers should be equipped with life jackets and the boat should carry flares, a spare oar, a compass, some means of baling out the boat, a spare sparking plug and pull rope for the outboard motor and if spare fuel is carried aboard take a funnel so that petrol spillage is minimised when refuelling at sea.

Although most dinghy anglers rarely venture more than two or three miles out to sea, tides and currents can still be dangerous.

Bad weather can envelope the angler in a matter of minutes and if in doubt, up anchor and head for home. Drifting can be a productive way of catching fish but it can also be dangerous near a rocky shoreline or when there are other craft about.

When hiring a charter boat the angler is well advised to check with the skipper that the boat carries safety equipment. If it does not, do not put to sea with him.

When it comes to safety matters at sea or a decision about turning back to harbour in the face of bad weather, the skipper's word is law. Obey the safety laws and you will enjoy your fishing.

Boat fishing can be a tiring business when the fish are coming fast. The choice of correct equipment is essential. This angler has invested in a butt harness to steady the rod when playing heavy fish. The harness is strapped round the waist to give both added leverage to the rod and protecting the angler from injury. Note the tremendous curve and power of the rod.

Pier fishing

For the sea angling beginner there can be few more pleasant ways of learning techniques and catching fish in the process than pier fishing.

Piers attract and hold fish the whole year round, giving the pier angler a chance to try his hand at all kinds of species from summer mackerel to winter cod.

Although many of the piers around our coastline have fallen into disrepair and are now being closed, pier anglers are taking an increasing number of specimen fish each year.

There are two types of pier—the pleasure pier, built on iron piles; and the walled pier, built to shelter harbours.

The pleasure pier

The pleasure pier provides easier fishing for the beginner. The tide runs freely through the piles and presents little problem to the angler.

In summer the main pier species are mackerel, bass, mullet, pouting, garfish and flatfish with the possibility of conger eels. In winter only the flatfish remain with the mackerel, mullet and bass shoals being replaced by shoals of cod and whiting.

Summer pier fishing offers the angler a variety of tactics from which to choose. He can spin or feather for mackerel and garfish; floatfish for mullet, mackerel and bass; or leger for the bottom feeding species like the dabs, rays and eels.

As with freshwater fishing, fish shoals congregate where the food supply is greatest and a knowledge of these likely 'holding spots' will increase the angler's catch.

Never be afraid to ask advice from regular anglers and whenever possible study the area around the pier at low tide, taking note of rocky patches, gullies and inlets which provide natural larders for fish.

Fish shoals are never far from the pier structure so long casting is unnecessary. A cast of 25 yards is quite sufficient and this can be achieved with either the fixed spool reel or centre pin reel. Long rods are a handicap for some kinds of pier fishing but at all costs avoid short, heavy, solid-glass 'pier rods'. A 12 foot beach-caster is adequate for most kinds of pier fishing and in summer for the smaller species, the angler can use a 10 foot freshwater carp rod.

Fish, especially bass, often congregate right among the girders and piles of the pier itself. Fishing among the ironwork can be a very productive method but tackle must be strong enough to hold a fish immediately it is hooked. Never fish this method with more than one hook—many good fish have been lost when the second hook has snagged an obstruction.

One of the most vital pieces of pier angling equipment is the dropnet. On many piers it is the only way of landing a big fish without breakage.

Use a round or near round weight with this method, and avoid grapnels or other leads with trailing pieces which are likely to snag on obstruction.

Baits can vary from ragworm, lugworm, fish strips, live fish and shellfish, although experience will soon teach the beginner the most productive bait from his particular pier.

For mid-water feeding species in summer, float fishing can often prove a deadly method. A sliding float, stopped by a bead and weighted by a spiral lead will allow the bait to be fished attractively in mid water, taking advantage of the tidal movement around the pier to search out the fish.

Floatfishing with a fixed float will allow the angler to use conventional bottom gear to search out the bottom feeding species.

Pleasure piers do allow the angler to use paternoster rigs to introduce variation into his fishing. A simple French boom paternoster rig with wire arms can be fished to deadly effect in summer. The arms can be adjusted to different depths so that one bait can be fished on the bottom and a second bait several feet higher in the water. The angler can experiment with long flowing traces in his efforts to seek out the fish, confident in the knowledge that he is unlikely to tangle with other anglers' lines.

The walled pier

The walled pier presents different problems. Its structure creates very strong tides at high water and incorrect casting and the use of unsuitable end tackle can lead to crossed lines. Simple paternoster rigs are ideal but do avoid long flowing traces. Grip leads are essential if tangles are to be avoided but choose leads with short wires. Grip leads with wires that are too long can anchor the bait too firmly on the bottom, making it difficult for the angler to spot bites.

Winter fishing from piers is mainly confined to cod and whiting, with the occasional flatfish. High water is

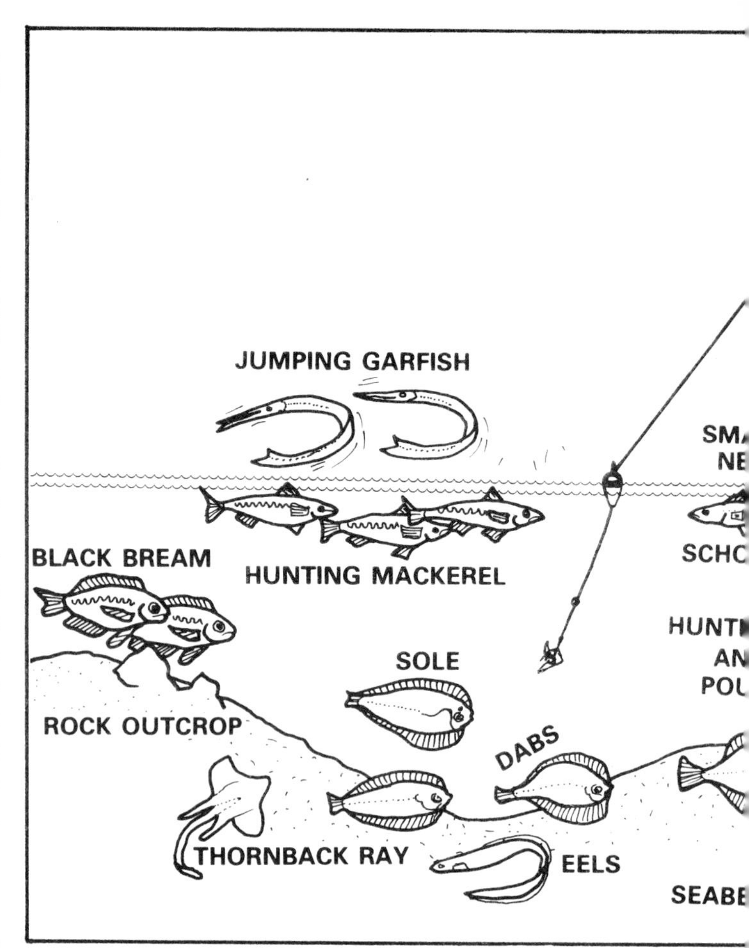

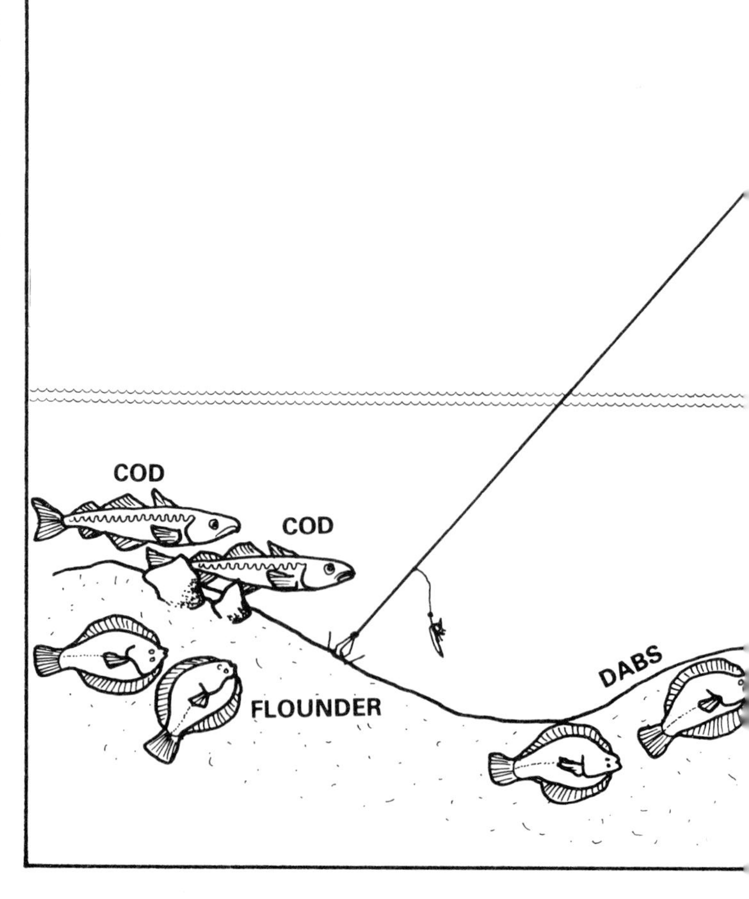

Summer and winter fishing presents two completely different challenges to the pier angler. In summer (above) the pier structure is a holding ground for all kinds of fish. Mackerel and garfish abound in the upper layers and can often be caught by spinning with light gear or light floatfishing; small pouting offer sport to the rawest novice; school bass and occasionally specimen bass are often to be found right among the pier's ironwork and the bottom fish can usually tempt tasty plaice, dabs and thornbacks.

In winter (below) the picture changes dramatically. Many of the summer species have disappeared completely. Only the flatfish remain from summer. But the pier angler's main target is now the cod and whiting shoals which forage inland after the first winter frosts and gales.

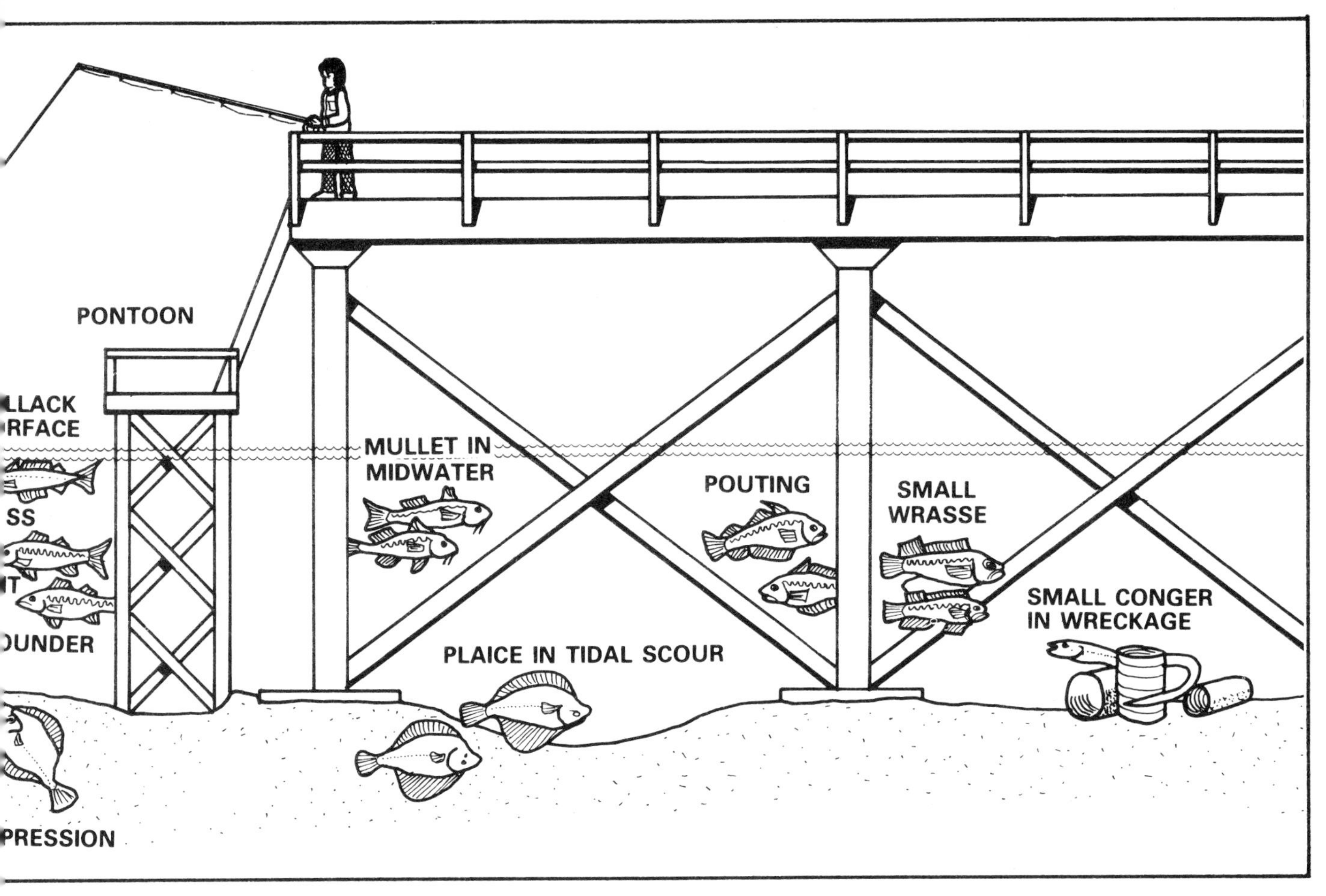
PONTOON
LLACK
RFACE
SS
OUNDER
PRESSION
MULLET IN
MIDWATER
POUTING
SMALL
WRASSE
SMALL CONGER
IN WRECKAGE
PLAICE IN TIDAL SCOUR

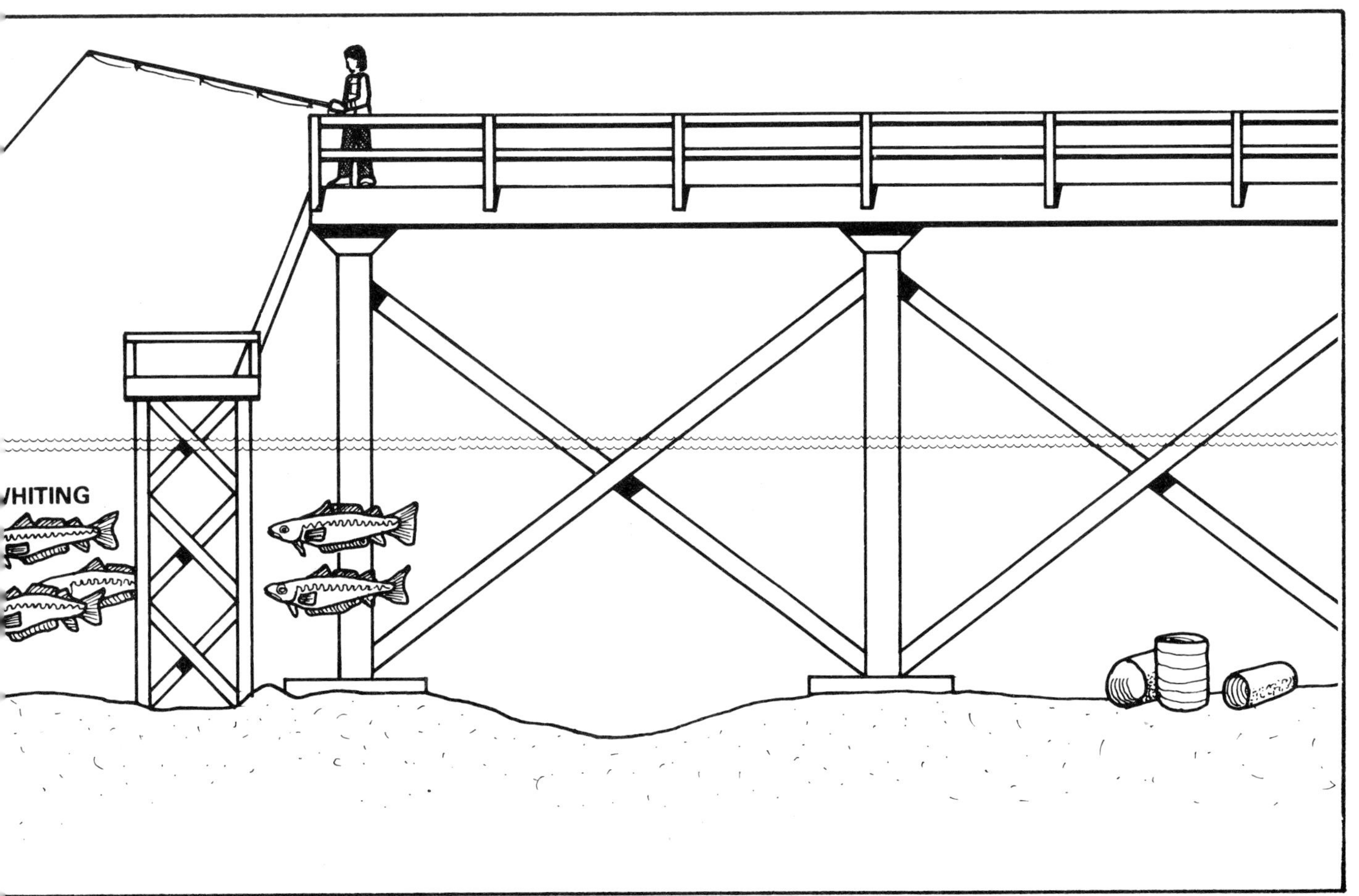
HITING

the best time for these fish, especially if it coincides with nightfall. Tackle must be strong enough to handle fish that may run to 20 or 30lb and lines should be in the 20-30lb breaking strain range. Terminal tackle should be kept as simple as possible but make sure that top quality hooks are attached. The strain of landing a big cod from a wave buffeted pier can put a tremendous demand on a hookhold.

Lugworm is one of the best winter cod baits, several worms being threaded on a 1/0 hook. Cocktail baits have accounted for many big pier cod as have squid, herring and shellfish baits.

Big cod will usually pick up a bait and keep on going making it an easy matter for the angler to drive home the hook. Smaller cod and whiting will attack the bait in short bursts producing a series of sharp taps on the rod top. Fierce bites often result in missed strikes and the angler should wait until a series of taps develops before striking.

Landing big fish from a pier calls for the use of a

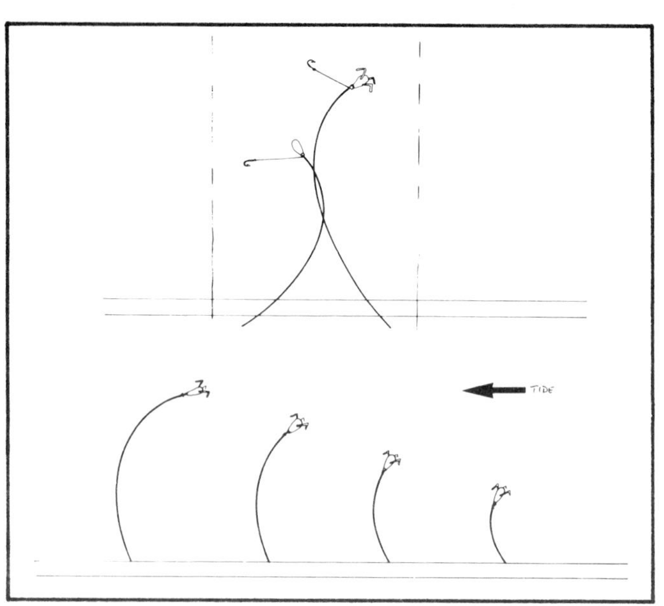

Correct casting from a crowded pier is essential if tangles and arguments are to be avoided. The angler on the uptide should cast shorter than the man downtide and so on.

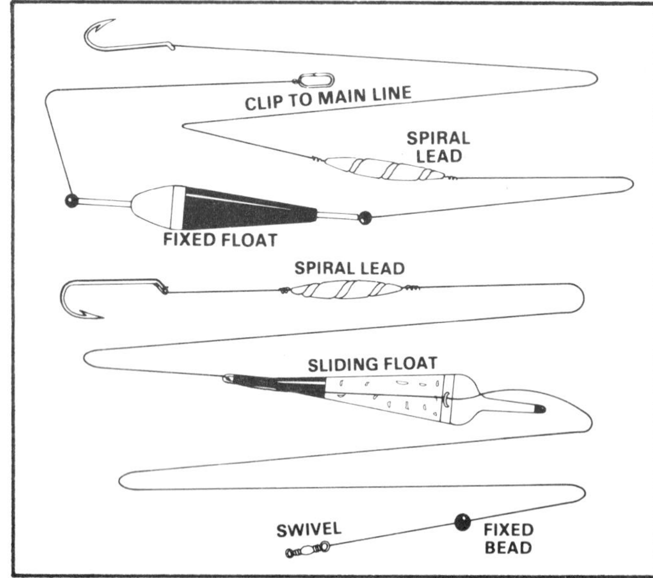

Float fishing, especially in summer, can be a deadly way of taking fish from the pier. The angler can use either the fixed float, stopped by split shot, to fish the bait just beneath the surface or at midwater (top illustration); or he can use a sliding float, to fish his bait on or near the bottom (bottom illustration).

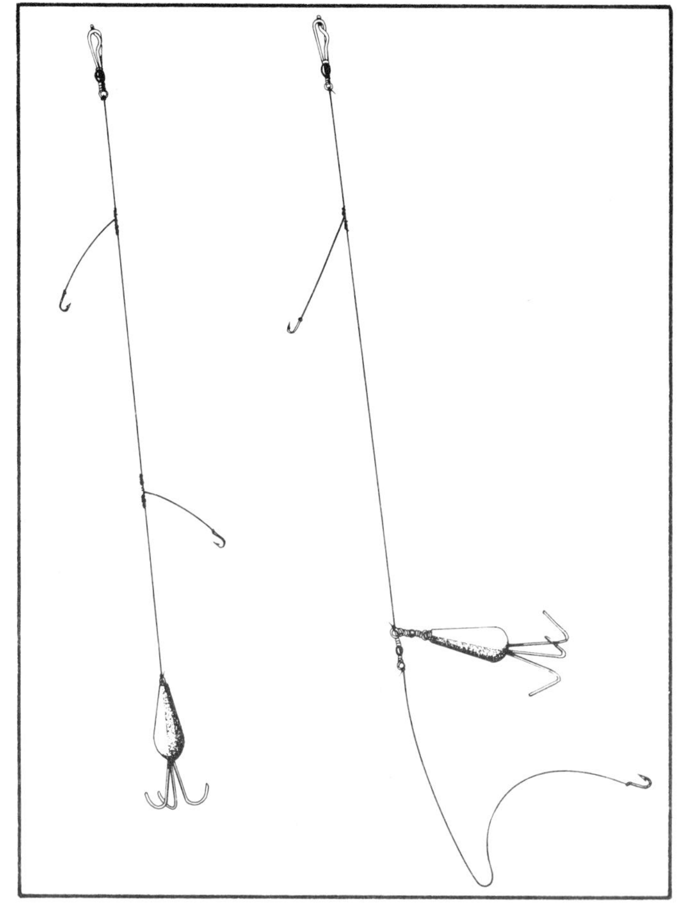

With pier fish often feeding at different depths or on different kinds of food it often pays to use two hooks to vary both presentation and bait. The two end rigs above are quick and easy to assemble and unlikely to cause tangles when casting.

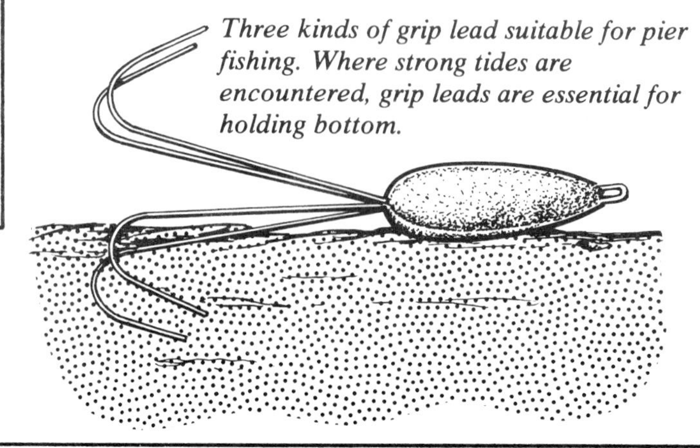

Three kinds of grip lead suitable for pier fishing. Where strong tides are encountered, grip leads are essential for holding bottom.

dropnet—a deep mesh attached to a large circular frame, like a bicycle wheel which can be lowered by rope from the pier to the water's edge. It is a good idea to attach a leadweight to the bottom of the net to give it stability in windy weather. Landing fish with the dropnet is a simple matter—provided the angler takes his time.

Wait until the fish is over the rim of the net before lifting and do not stab at it whenever it is within range.

After a day's pier fishing always clear up after you. Do not leave litter, pieces of unwanted line or left-over bait on the pier. Many yards of good pier fishing have been lost to anglers because of such carelessness. All small and undersized fish should be returned to the sea as soon as they are unhooked.

There are few more pathetic sights than hand-sized flatfish, destined for the dustbin, gasping out their last breaths on the pier planks. If fish are too small for eating return them to the sea—they may one day grow to specimen size.

When the tide is flowing towards the pier angler, fish taking his bait will tend to continue swimming with the tide towards the pier. The bite will not be signalled by a downward movement of the rod tip but by the line slackening in a pronounced fashion. Take up the slack and strike the hook home.

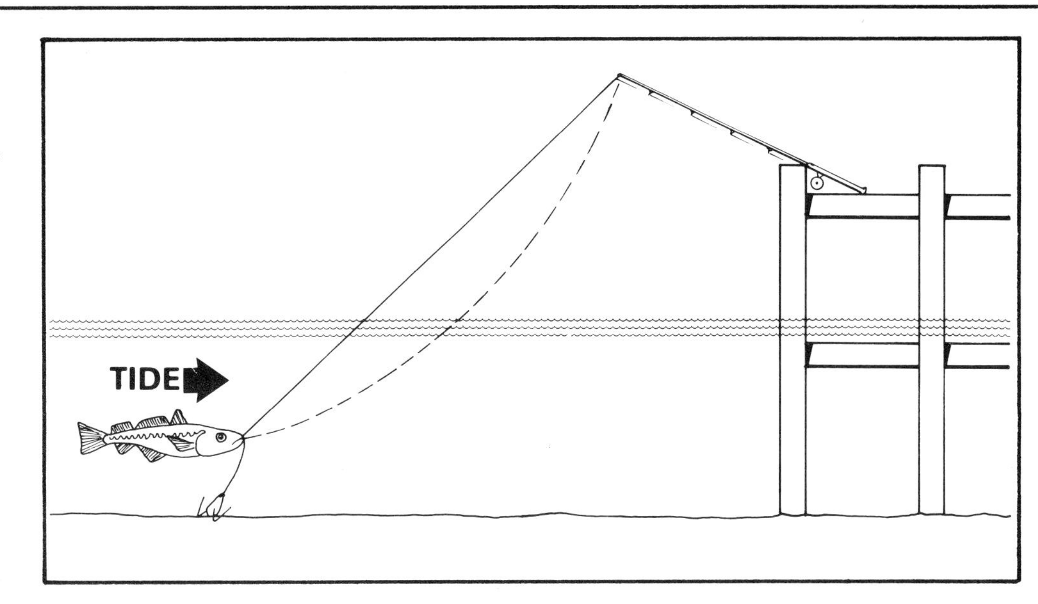

When the tide is flowing away from the angler biting fish will move away with the tide after taking the bait. The bite will be signalled by a definite downward movement of the rod top.

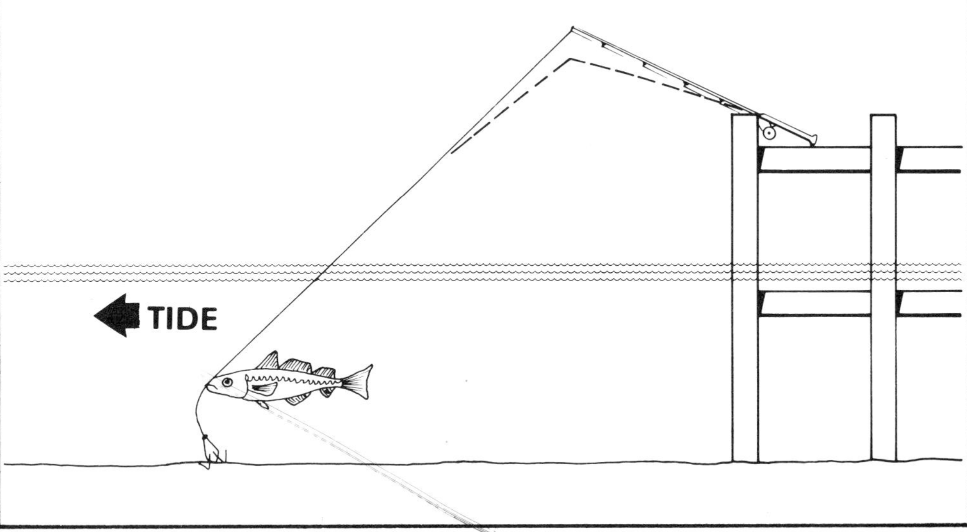

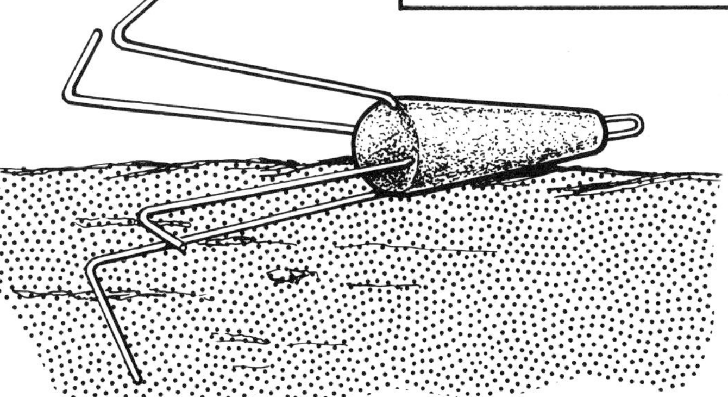

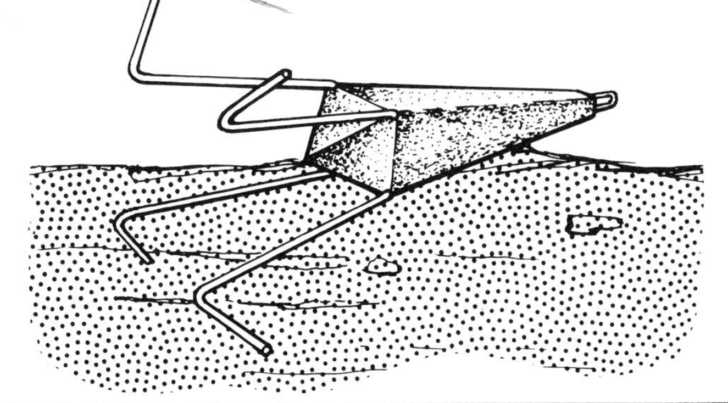

Sea floats

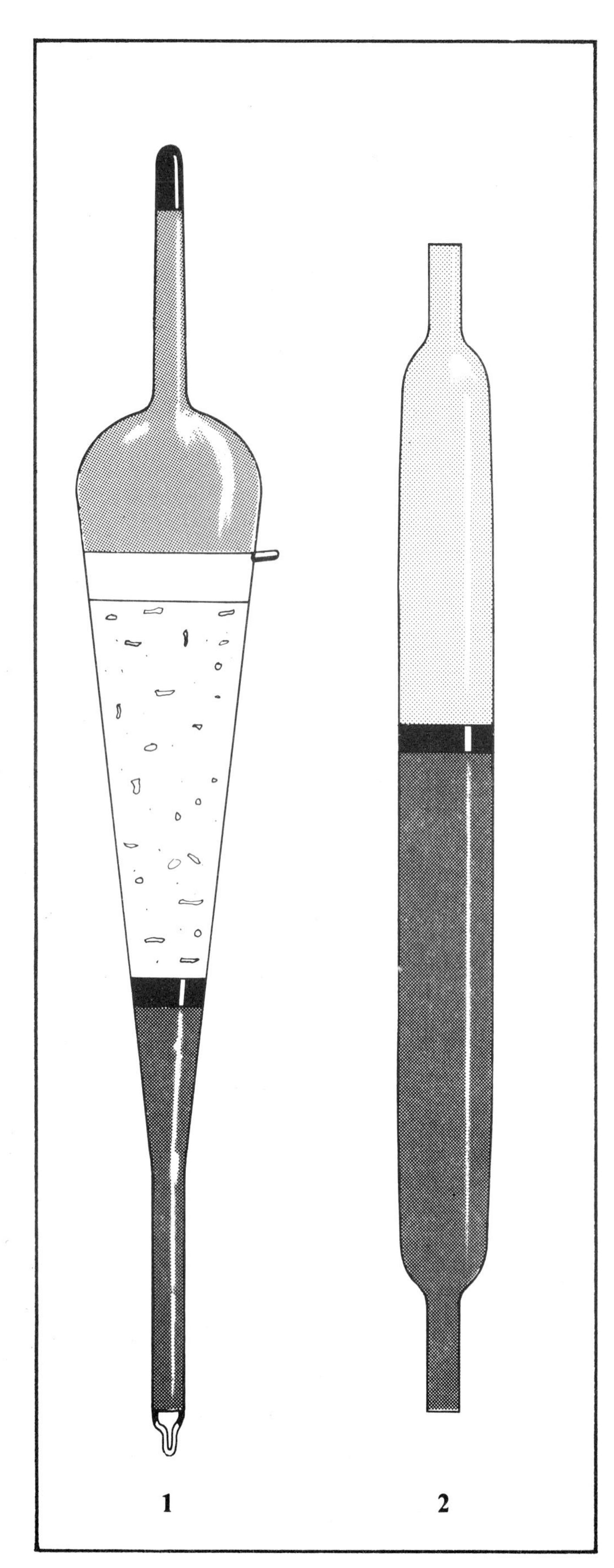

In the calm, bright conditions of summer, predatory sea fish, such as mackerel, bass and pollack hunt for food off the bottom. So the ideal way of catching them is with a float.

Sea floats are generally sliders of one sort of another. This allows the tackle to be cast well out to fish deep water. The float can either slide up the line by rings on the side or through a plastic tube in the centre of the float. A stop-knot or rubber band can be used to fix the float at the depth required. But remember to use beads either side of the float to ensure the stop-knot does not pull through the ring or tube.

You will need a brightly painted top to see the float at distance, but do not make the mistake of using a float big enough to moor a battleship. A small fish will never pull it under even though it may try.

A slim balsa float able to carry up an ounce of lead is ideal. Weight the float according to conditions. If the surface is ruffled you will need to have plenty of float above the water. Otherwise you will not see it. Under calm conditions it pays to weight the float so that only the tip is showing.

Do not expect the float to disappear and keep going. Bites from fish like pollack and wrasse are often very quick and need to be struck immediately. Always keep a tight line to the float and make sure the line floats.

A bait fished in the top 12 feet of water might catch bass, garfish, mullet, pollack and mackerel. Choose a rock or pier where the float can be paid out into the tide. The weight should be halfway down the line or less to allow attractive movement of the bait. It is important to use a fixed lead. A lead sliding up and down can lead to tangles in casting. Some anglers prefer a spiral, others a Wye spinning lead with a swivel at one end. Another way is to lock a barrel lead on the line with swivels at either end.

Pier anglers fishing on the bottom often clip on a separate float tackle to their main line and slide it down to the water in 'ski lift' fashion. This way they can fish the top and the bottom at the same time.

Fishing rock marks may call for a bigger float as the water tends to be boily, pulling the float round in the turmoil of currents. The weight of the heavier float can also be useful in casting and it may need to support a large bait such as a small pouting if the quarry is bass. So match float size to conditions.

Left: Figure 1 shows a heavy cork slider with a ring on the side for the line. Use for distance casting for bass and pollack in deepish water. Figure 2 is a slender balsa slider where the line travels through the centre of the float. It is ideal for mackerel, garfish and mullet.

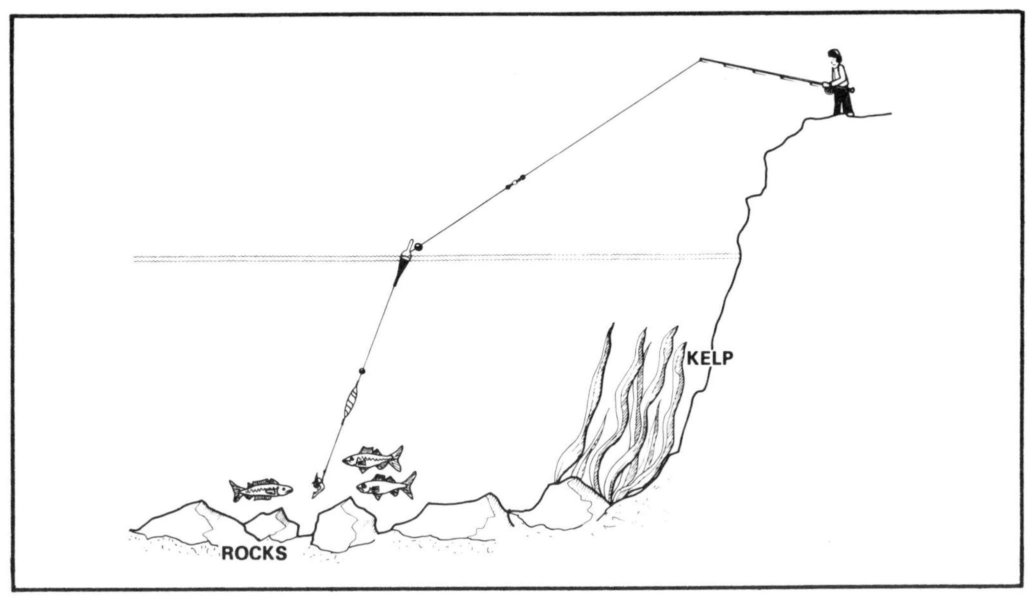

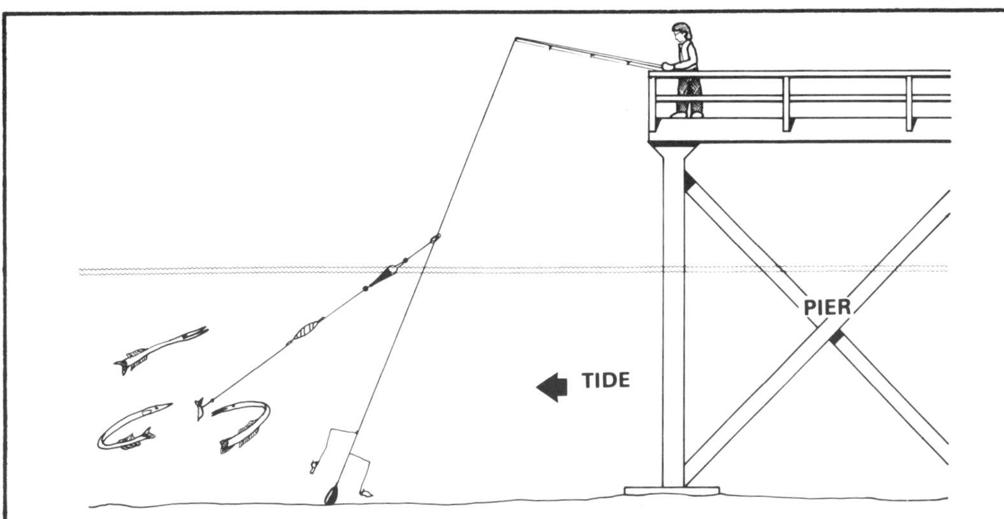

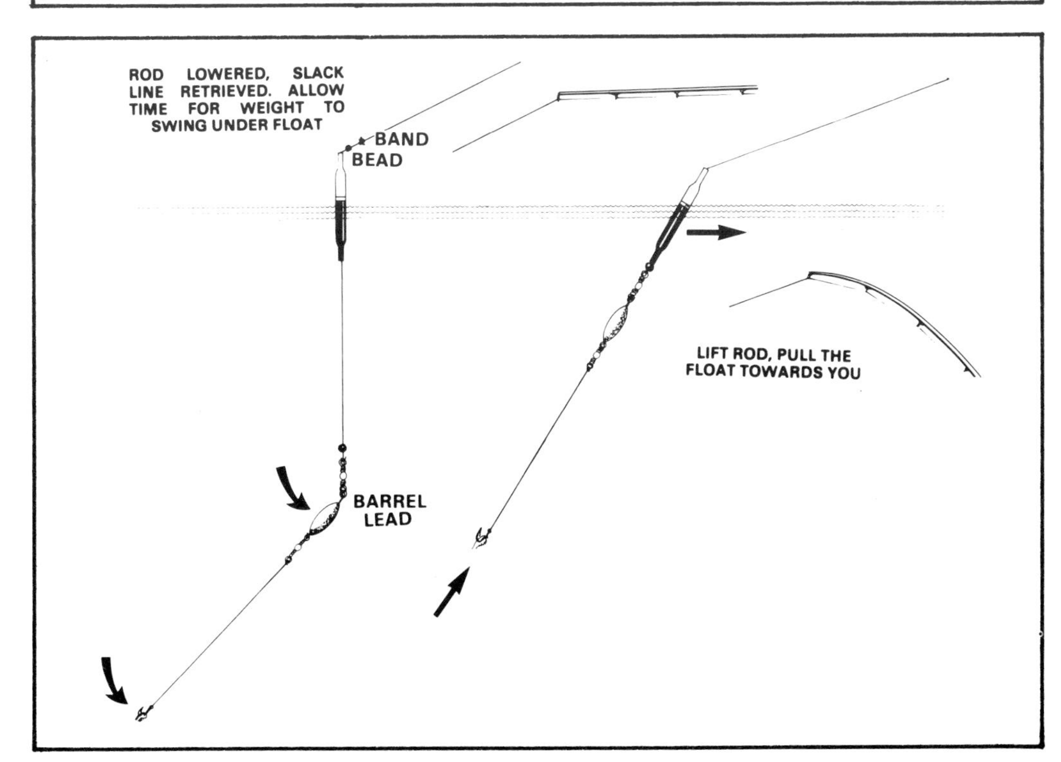

Top: The cork slider at work over rocky ground. Here the float has been stopped by a bead fixed on the line. But it could have been a stopknot. The position of the spiral lead is important . . . too high and the bait misses the fish, too low and the angler snags up.

Centre: This float rig for the upper layer is slid 'ski fashion' down the angler's line to pay out in the tide. Expect garfish, mullet and mackerel on this tackle.

Left: Use this method of retrieving with the float for bass, garfish and mackerel. Float is the pencil balsa with the line travelling through its centre. Weight is a barrel lead fixed at both ends by two swivels. Keep the lead at least five feet away from the hook. Pay the float out in the current and then retrieve it slowly back so that the bait works at different depths. The float is stopped on the line by a rubber band with the ends trimmed.

Cod

Few other sea fish can claim the almost magical aura of the cod. Ugly, ungainly, sometimes undramatic in fighting qualities—yet what other fish draws thousands of anglers every winter to cold, dark beaches? Open to all the hostile elements of winter on the exposed sands and shingle, the cod angler does not complain. He is wrapped up in the charisma of his quarry.

Boat anglers, too endure the roughest seas for their succession of codling, hoping all the time for that highly-prized 20-pounder or more. No other sea fish can equal the widespread, and intense, adoration from anglers, that this pot-bellied, huge mouthed and dirty-coloured creature receives.

Techniques

Cod can be taken from the shore or boats, but methods vary vastly in different parts of the country. The sand and shingle beaches of the east and south-east coasts, from Norfolk to Sussex attract beach anglers in their thousands during autumn and winter. In these areas, the further you can cast the better. Most fish come in close on night tides.

Lugworm baits are hurled towards the Continent with 11ft or 12ft beachcasters capable of casting 4–6oz of lead well over 100 yards.

Multipliers are the most common reel used, and line strength can vary from 18lb to 30lb, though more anglers are turning to lines as light as 12lb. This enables them to cast further and gives far more sport from the plunging fish.

Because of the immense strains placed on the last few yards of line during the cast, beach anglers use a 'shock leader' of much stronger line, as much as 40lb or more, to take the strain. This should be the length of your rod, plus a few turns on the reel.

Southern cod men favour a short paternoster holding the hook, with the lead clipped to the end of the shock leader. In the north, such light tackle would not survive a single cast. The sea bed there is a mass of rocks, gullies and kelp beds. Northern anglers use lines of 60–80lb breaking-strain, big strong centre-pin reels, and 'rotten bottoms'. A rotten bottom is a link of much lighter line holding the weight, so that you can break away from a snag, keeping your main line carrying the hook and fish.

Boat anglers all over the country favour a flowing trace. The main line is passed through a Clements boom which holds the weight. The boom is stopped by a swivel at the required distance from the hook—anything from a few feet to 10ft, depending on the tide.

Another popular northern method for cod is to use the pirk, a heavy chromed lure that is dropped and then retrieved from the sea bed. White feathers can be used in a similar way. Pirks are also used by wreck anglers after cod in the south, and on certain specialised cod marks like the Varne Bank, off Kent. Pirks are particularly popular in the deep Scottish sea lochs, where you may be fishing in anything up to 60 fathoms. Old-fashioned steel-boomed paternoster rigs are dying out rapidly. The big move is towards lighter tackle.

When to fish

Anglers in the North-east and Scotland have an almost exclusive ticket to fish for the small red rock cod all summer. Almost exclusive, because a few big cod are also caught from Cornish and Devon wreck marks. However, the real cod season—that time of year that sends a thrill through the blood of cod men everywhere—is the winter. Cod spawn in the three months after Christmas, in deep-water marks well offshore.

In the autumn the fish come well inshore to enjoy the rich pickings of natural food such as whiting, sprats and crabs; the main cod-catching areas are the east and south-east coasts, from Norfolk to Sussex. Boat anglers cash in as well, usually taking a better stamp of fish. In the north as well, better quality cod move in—especially in the Scottish west coast sea lochs, where they go to spawn. It is from marks like the Gantocks on the Firth of Clyde, that most of the really big fish are taken.

Location

There are few places on Britain's coast where cod are not found. The North-east and Scottish coasts hold vast numbers of small 'rock' cod, running to a few pounds, all the year round. In autumn and winter the bigger fish move in inshore to marks such as the deep Scottish sea lochs where they spawn. The Firth of Clyde and Loch Long are highly rated. North Sea cod are caught all along the east and south-east coast as they migrate southwards to spawn, from the end of October onwards.

Big cod are also caught in water off the Isle of Wight and in the Bristol Channel. During summer Devon and Cornwall produce some very big fish over deepwater wrecks while big catches of medium-sized fish come from isolated wreck and sand-banks off the Kent coast. The Varne Bank is one example.

Baits

These vary a great deal depending on the area. The only guideline is that the baits should be big. Lugworm is the best known and most widely-used bait, with a following all over the country. Ragworm is used, too, but in the northern waters of Scotland, Northumberland, and north Yorkshire, anglers pin a lot of faith in pirks—heavy artificial lures. They work well in the clear water, though are not so effective in murky water further south. Northerners also rate mussel highly for the smaller rock cod, and peeler crab which they can use for cod all summer.

Boat anglers find squid one of their best baits, and often use it in conjunction with lugworm to make a cocktail. Sprats and herring are used to take cod when they are chasing shoals of bait fish. A small whiting left on a hook will often take the best cod of all.

Bass

The bass is surely the most striking of all our British sea fish. With a powerful, heavy-set body, fierce head and spined fins all too ready to bristle in anger, it looks and acts, like the king of the sea.

The bass is an aggressive fish, with a savage bite, and its long, powerful runs signal the start of a hectic battle for boat and shore angler alike. Although it is known to grow well in excess of 20lb, the average can run anywhere from a few pounds up to low double figures depending on the locality.

Techniques

The bass is an aggressive hunter spending much of its time chasing small fish. So spinning from boat or shore is one of the most effective methods of taking them. Choose a heavy spinner that casts well, such as the Toby or German sprat. Artificial eels such as the Redgill or Eddystone can be even more effective. These are best trolled at slow speed behind a boat high up in the water.

For lure fishing from the shore, look for a headland where the water races round and cast into the heaviest water. Cast along the shore and retrieve parallel to the rocks. Be ready for a savage take. If you are fishing over very rough ground, try the sliding float. Bait could be prawn, soft-back crab, king ragworm or a strip of sandeel.

The method most likely to produce the really big bass is legering over rough ground, where sand blends into rock and weed growth is plentiful. Here, solitary big fish will be scavenging for crabs, eels, small fish and, at times, squid or cuttlefish that have been washed in.

A survey of such an area at low tide will show you the places to avoid and the sandy, clear areas to cast to. Choose mackerel or herring for the biggest fish. Apply similar preparation to open storm beaches. They may seem featureless, but these venues often have gullies or freshwater streams.

Bass are powerful fighters, but can be held on fairly light tackle for maximum sport. Long rods are needed to exert pressure on the running fish and for ease of casting. Lines should be around 12lb from the shore.

Locations

The bass is essentially a warm-water species, most widespread along the south and west shores of Britain. Expect to catch them in some numbers from the Suffolk coast right round the coast to North Wales. Further north, the Irish and North seas still hold bass, but in smaller numbers.

Bass love brackish water and will often move some distance up rivers. Harbour jetties or moorings in tidal rivers are favourite bass marks during summer. In autumn the deeper shingle beaches like Chesil attract the bigger fish.

The successful bass angler will not need to cast far, for the bass will move in very close to the shore after shrimps, crabs and small flatfish under cover of darkness. If there is a good surf running after a summer storm, a crab bait should be fished just beyond the breakers. In calmer weather the bass shoal up after sandeels and brit. Then big boat catches can be made using artificial lures.

The hunting bass will range over all types of ground—sand, shingle and rock—in its search for food. Rocky, broken ground with deep, sandy gullies, as at Sussex's Beachy Head or Charmouth in Dorset, are favourite bass marks.

This type of rugged terrain will produce those highly-prized double-figure fish. The more open, sandy beaches or river mouths are usually full of the smaller school bass. In autumn and winter bass shoal up in vast concentrations over deep-water marks.

Plymouth's Eddystone Reef probably holds the largest bass shoals in the country, with many thousands of fish concentrated into a small area. Over rock marks near the Eddystone or Manacles, bass feed high up in

the water on sprats, pilchards and brit. At dawn and dusk they will splash and break the surface in their hunt for food. However, in shallow, broken water, like the surf beaches of North Cornwall, fish will nose in the sand.

Bass seem attracted to underwater obstructions such as wrecks, harbour walls or pier pilings—where they play and frolic in full view of anglers.

When to fish

In Spring the small school bass appear inshore in estuaries and river mouths. As the year wears on, the schools break up leaving solitary bass to roam inshore shallows. In warm weather bass will move into a few feet of water hunting crabs and prawns. An on-shore wind sends them into the surf, especially on the first of the flood. When the sea is calm and clear, the bass shoal up to harry sandeel, brit and other small fish.

By the end of November the bass tend to move off-shore where they shoal in vast numbers. Some fish still stay inshore during the winter, where they can provide some sport for the shore angler. The movements and breeding habits of the bass are still somewhat of a mystery. Spawning is thought to take place in deep water, but eggs and young fish have also been found in estuaries. The bass is a slow-growing species and does not mature until it is at least five years old.

Baits

Bass are very accommodating fish. They can be taken on a wide variety of baits and methods including legering, floatfishing, spinning and live-baiting.

Small 'school' bass of a pound or two feed on crustaceans, worms and small fish. Bigger bass have more bulk to satisfy. As well as the food of their younger brethren, they readily chase sandeels, sprats and even mackerel. Soft-back crab, live prawns, squid, razor-fish and mackerel fillets are great favourites with bass anglers. A popular bait for really big fish is a live pouting or mackerel.

In the West Country, a live sandeel is the most effective bait for bass, but if you cannot get hold of the real thing, artificial eels—like the Redgill—can be just as effective. Other top bass lures are the Toby and German sprat.

Plaice

If the mighty halibut is the king of flatfish, then the handsome plaice is certainly the prince. Those orange spots have delighted anglers from South Coast pier heads to Scottish sea lochs. For not only does the plaice eat well, but it is also a strong fighter.

Techniques

Plaice, like all flatfish, spend much of their life lying hidden in the sea bed sand. The only movement will be a puff of sand as the gill cover rises and falls. But should a tasty sandeel or shrimp swim past without spotting those two stalkish eyes the camouflaged plaice can leave its hideout in a second to grab its prey.

Most plaice from the shore are caught on standard bottom gear baited with lug or ragworm. But to catch the bigger fish you need to go afloat. The most effective method is to use a long running trace baited with king ragworm, or a strip of sandeel. This works in the tide creating an enticing moving bait. If you are not anchored over a noted plaice mark, drift the boat across a sandy bottom to cover the ground. Plaice are curious about movement, so it pays to keep that bait moving. Drifting makes the lead puff up little spurts of sand, which attracts the plaice.

Many anglers go one step further and use plastic or metal spoons baited with worm. The plaice perhaps believes the spoon is a smaller flattie making off with the bait, so it chases and intercepts. Several brightly-coloured beads on the trace can also make a difference. The lighter weight tackle you can use, the better. You will get more bites and a lot more action as the tip bends with a powerful plaice.

When to fish

In spring plaice are often thin and out of condition after spawning. But the spent fish soon fatten up in shallow water through the summer.

By autumn the fish are in peak condition and begin to work their way out to deeper water. It is then that the best fish of all are caught. By the end of December they have vanished to spawn. Plaice feed best in calm seas and clear water in periods of neap tides.

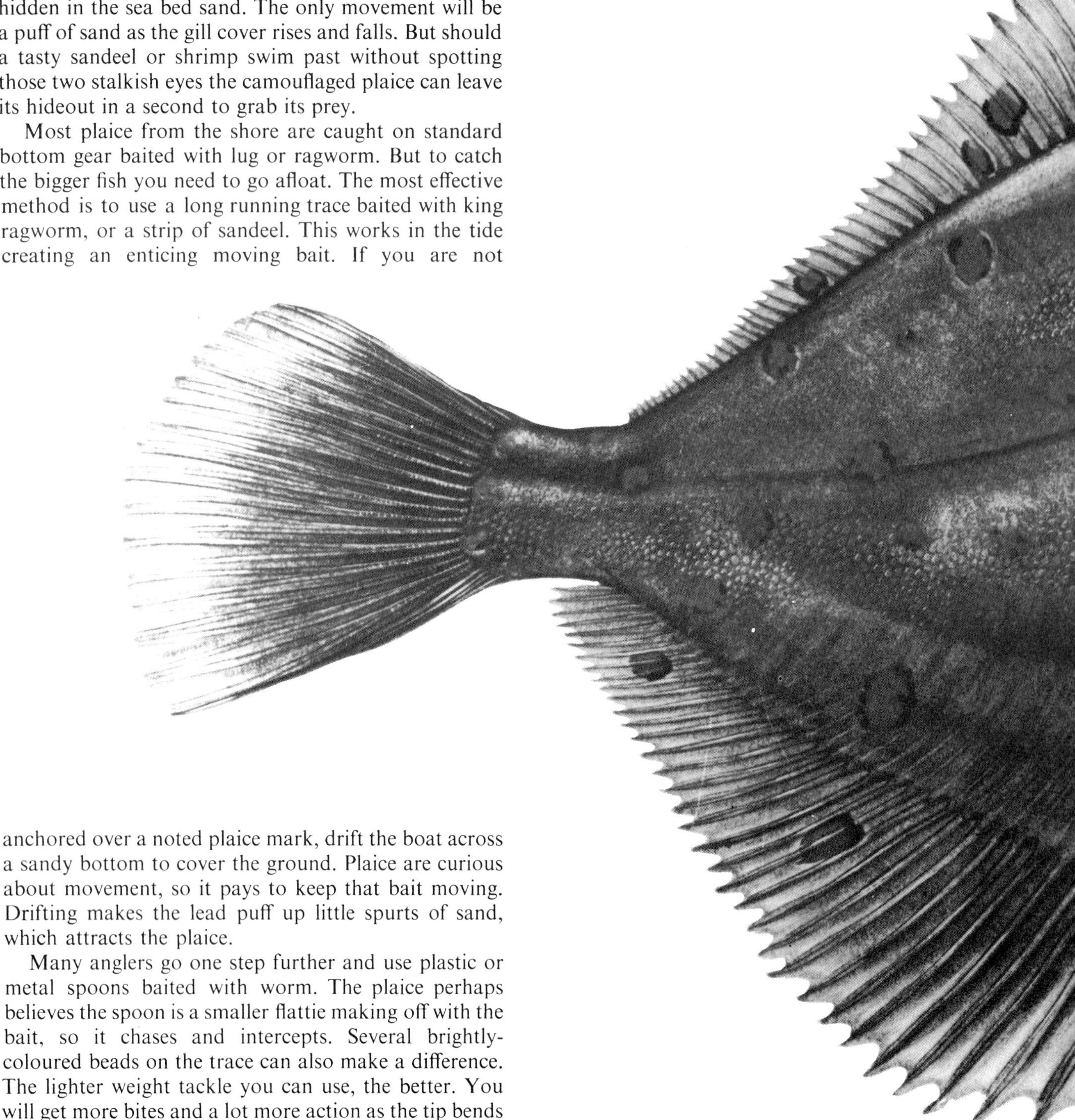

Location

The plaice is found right round our coasts. Small fish up to one or two pounds are caught by beach and pier anglers. But the bigger fish are found in deeper water. Best fishing spots are small pockets of sand protected by rocks and mussel beds.

Sandbanks such as the Skerries, in Devon, have provided huge hauls of specimen plaice in the past. But netting and diving has reduced stocks. The estuaries of the rivers Axe, Fowey and Teign regularly provide a crop of big fish. And Poole harbour still yields its fair share of five-pounders.

Portsmouth harbour has a reputation for good numbers of medium-sized plaice, while further east off Deal and Folkestone mussel beds attract large concentrations in spring. Off Bridlington, in Yorkshire, coble anglers catch big plaice.

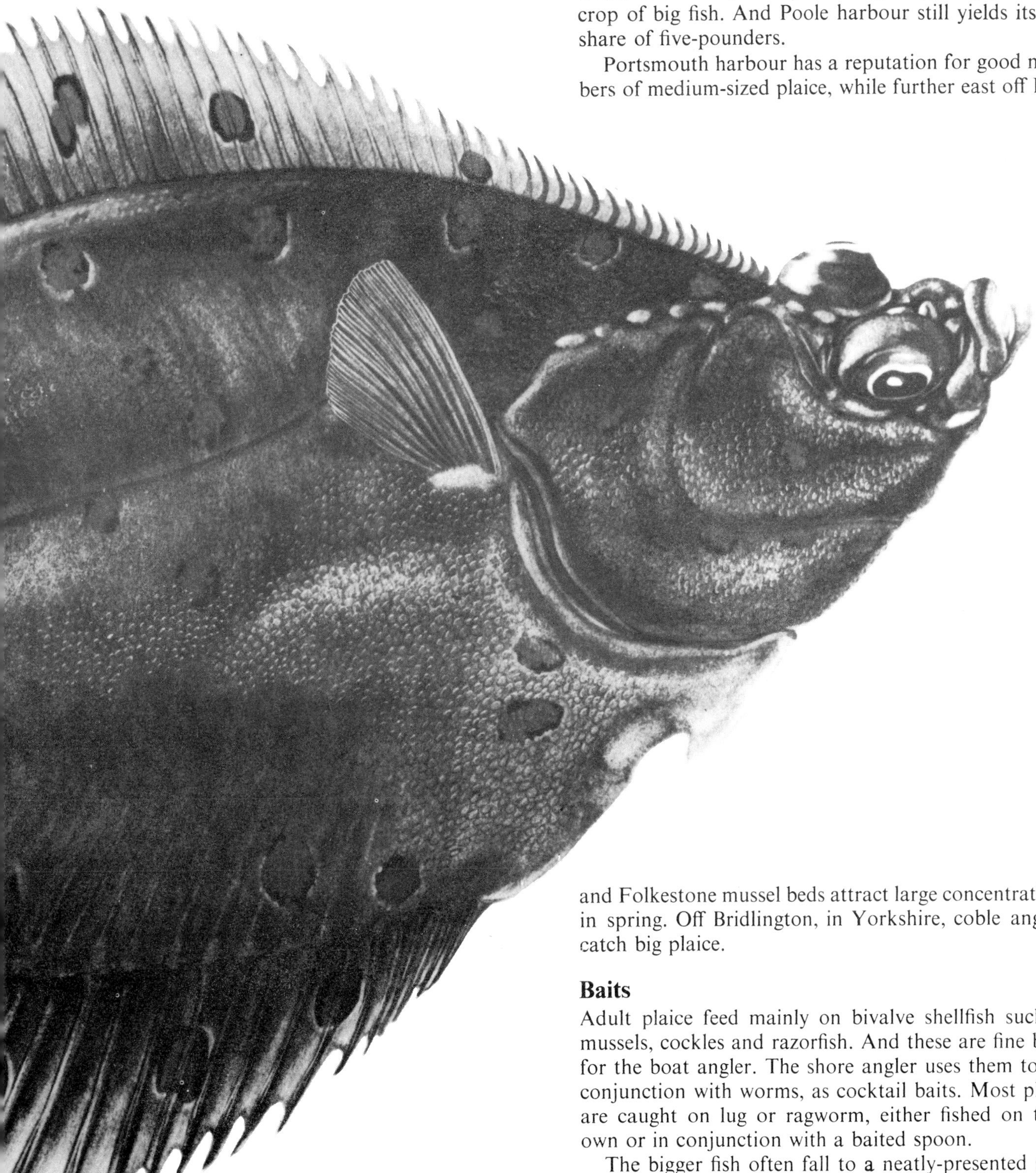

Baits

Adult plaice feed mainly on bivalve shellfish such as mussels, cockles and razorfish. And these are fine baits for the boat angler. The shore angler uses them too in conjunction with worms, as cocktail baits. Most plaice are caught on lug or ragworm, either fished on their own or in conjunction with a baited spoon.

The bigger fish often fall to a neatly-presented strip of sandeel or mackerel flesh drifted across the bottom. Peeler, hermit carb and squid will take plaice in early winter.

Tope

The tope is a member of the shark family displaying the same exciting fighting qualities of its larger brothers and sisters. For many anglers it is the largest and toughest opponent that they are likely to meet in their angling careers, and its widespread distribution makes it à popular sport fish for thousands of boat and shore fanatics.

Streamlined in shape, it is built for speed and acceleration, making long scorching runs when hooked. Mystery still surrounds the fish, but because it is of sporting and not economic importance, little scientific research has been carried out on the species. However, one specimen, tagged by the Irish Inland Fisheries Trust off Co. Clare, turned up two years later, 700 miles away off the coast of Northern Spain.

Techniques

A medium sea rod with a test curve in the 30-35lb range is ideal. Tope put up a tremendous fight on light gear but a reasonably powerfully actioned rod is often necessary to drive home the hooks at long range. Several hundred yards of 30-35lb line and a drum reel with a brake complete the tackle.

Hooks can range from 4/0 to 7/0 depending on the type of bait used. Leads, when boat fishing from the stern, should be as light as possible, just holding bottom.

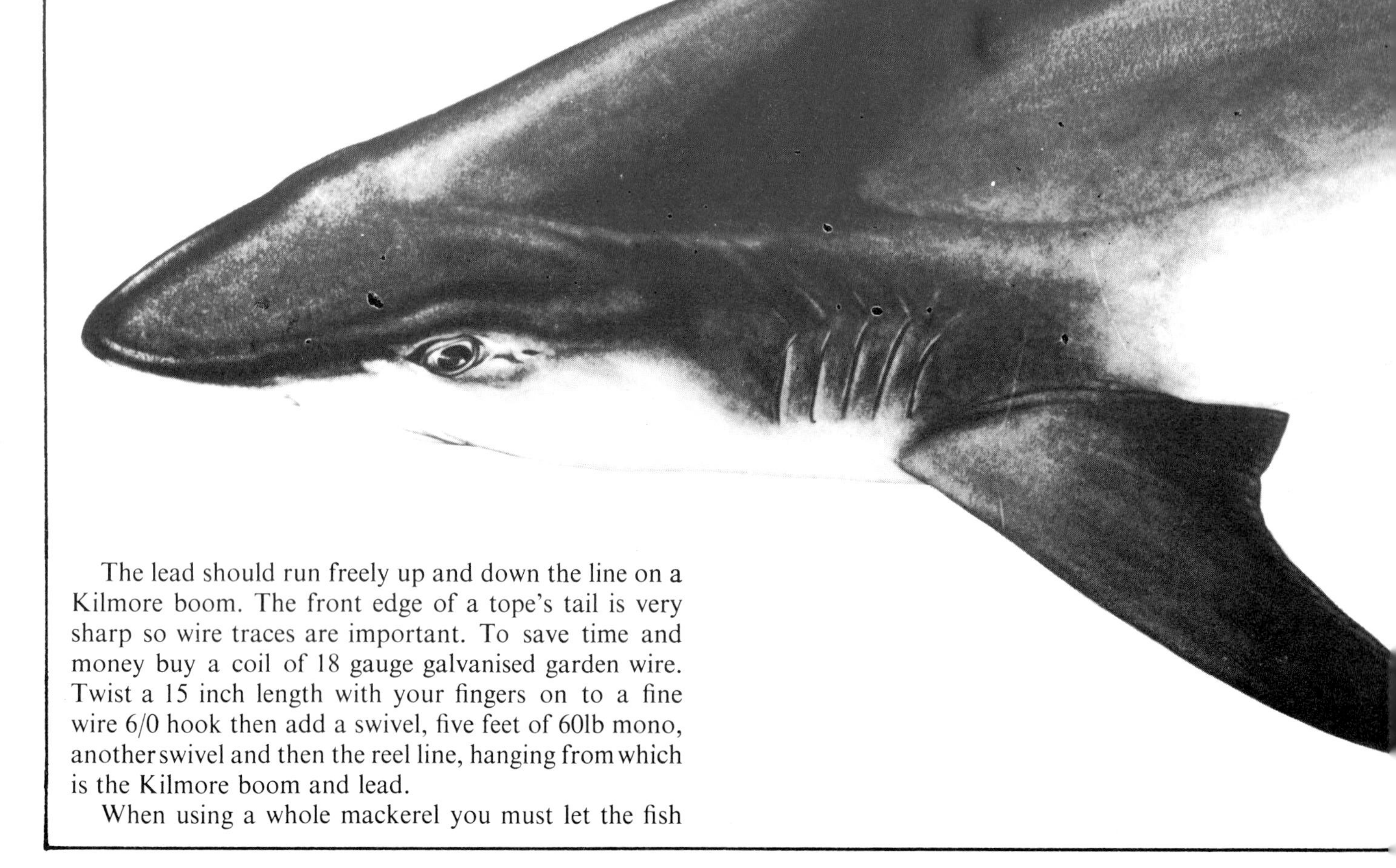

The lead should run freely up and down the line on a Kilmore boom. The front edge of a tope's tail is very sharp so wire traces are important. To save time and money buy a coil of 18 gauge galvanised garden wire. Twist a 15 inch length with your fingers on to a fine wire 6/0 hook then add a swivel, five feet of 60lb mono, another swivel and then the reel line, hanging from which is the Kilmore boom and lead.

When using a whole mackerel you must let the fish run. This initial run may be anything from 60-150 yards. When the second run develops it is time to tighten and drive the hook home with one long strike. By using a belly strip of mackerel the angler can turn his tackle into a virtual instant strike rig. The hook point is not masked and fish can be hit on the first run.

For beach tope, choose a strong beach-caster and multiplier capable of carrying 300 yards of 25lb line. Bites will be screaming runs, so set the drag light.

When to fish

Tope have been caught off our coast during every month of the year. But the main run of fish normally arrives at the end of April, staying as late as the end of October. The North Devon coast often produces the odd big fish in late October, well after the main run of fish has disappeared.

The tope is viviparous and the young, up to 40 in number, are born in shallow water in summer. The females run much larger than the males with the great majority of fish taken on rod and line being males. In some areas a rod-caught female is a rarity.

Location

Tope are widely distributed round the coasts of the British Isles and Ireland, with certain key areas where they are very common. Noted areas are the Wash; the mouth of the Thames Estuary; Littlehampton; the Solent; Carmarthen Bay, off the peninsulas of Pembrokeshire; Cardigan Bay; off North Wales; Morecambe Bay; Mull of Galloway; Co. Wexford, Ireland; Tralee Bay, Co. Kerry and the coasts of Donegal and Mayo.

The tope fishing in the Wash, superb in the early sixties, has now declined. But new hot spots, especially off the Welsh coast, are being discovered every year.

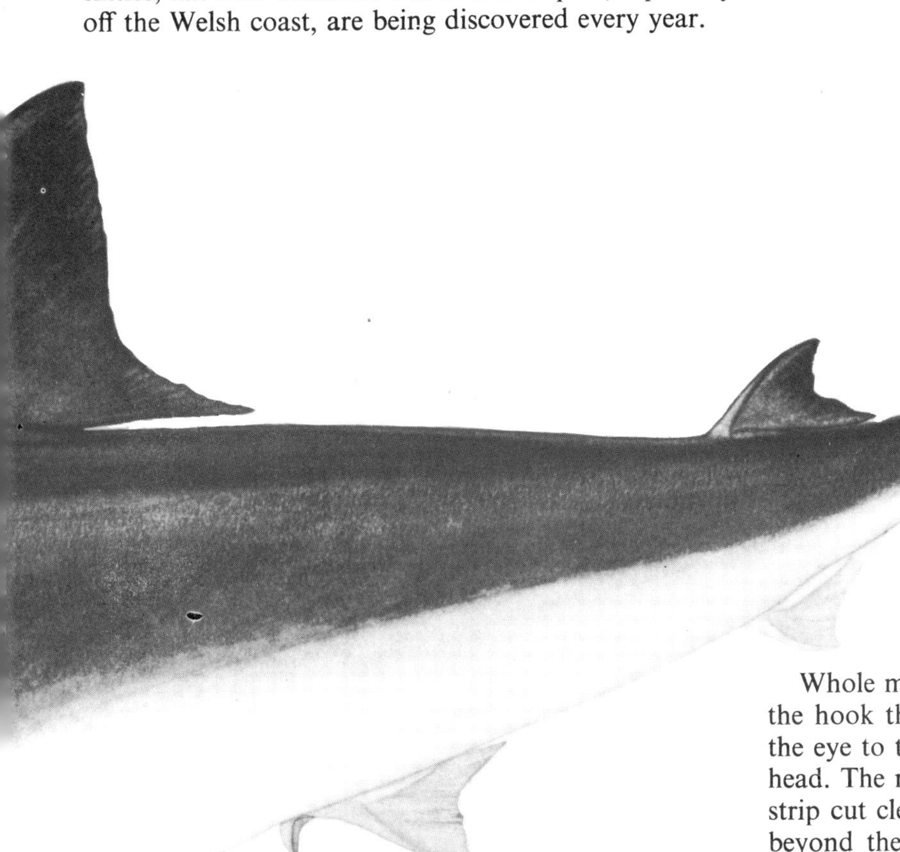

Two factors seem to govern the presence of inshore tope. A good tide run, usually found around estuary mouths or around an offshore race, is an essential ingredient. So too is the presence of large shoals of food fish like mackerel, herring or whiting. The presence of tope off Littlehampton for example, is largely due to the huge shoals of black bream in the area.

Tope are nearly always associated with clean sandy ground. But they are often found over rocky ground too, at times coming really close inshore, where they are caught by the shore angler equipped for tope. Trevose Head and other North Cornish headlands provide thrills with extra-big tope in late autumn.

Baits

Fresh bait is a must. Tope, like all members of the shark family, have a more highly developed sense of smell and taste than sight. Top bait is undoubtedly the mackerel. But herring, whiting and dabs also make superb baits.

Whole mackerel can be fished on a 6/0 by threading the hook through, with a baiting needle, from behind the eye to the tail so that the hook sits just behind the head. The most attractive part of a mackerel is a belly strip cut cleanly right through both sides from gills to beyond the vent. It is attractive, boneless and works well in the tide. Do not bunch it, but hang it on the hook by one end.

Whole dabs, often used by east coast and Kent anglers where they are in plentiful supply, are another superb bait. For fishing a fast tide push the hook in about two inches from the tail, through again and out just behind the head.

On slacker tides cut deep along the lateral line on the white side of the fish then fold it in half so the white side is showing. Put the hook in the head and pull it out into the white.

With their highly developed sense of smell, tope respond eagerly to 'ground-baiting'. Pulped up mackerel, placed in a string bag, and hung over the side of the boat will soon produce an ever-widening slick of oil and blood on which the fish can home in. Similarly cod-liver-oil, sprinkled in the water, can provide an attractive tope ground-bait for the shore angler in some selected areas.

Mullet

A flash of silver and the mullet is on. You have hooked the hardest-fighting fish for its size in the sea. There is no give-and-take when a mullet is battling for its freedom. The mullet steams off from the start demanding line, otherwise it will surely break. If the fight goes in your favour, you can be sure that the mullet has given everything.

Techniques

The mullet is an enigma. Shoaling boldly off harbour walls, piers and moorings in full view of anglers, it still remains one of the most difficult of all fish to catch. Tackle must be light and sensitive otherwise the mullet will just ignore your bait with contempt.

To catch mullet you must outwit the fish. Be prepared to change your tackle and bait to suit the occasion. It is the nearest thing to carp fishing to be found in the sea. When mullet are feeding in tidal rivers such as the Rother, Adur, Arun or Axe, normal freshwater float tackle is all you need. Keep the bait off the bottom and cast near where you expect the shoal to swim. If you cast on top of the fish you will just scare them away. On piers, harbours and jetties, tackle can be slightly heavier. A spinning or leger rod loaded with 7lb line supporting an ounce weight is what is needed. Fish the bait paternoster-fashion, off the main line.

Lower the lead straight down to the depth the mullet are feeding. Then watch the rod tip for that shy pull. A gentle lift and wait for the fireworks. To bring the mullet around lower a string bag in the water full of mashed bread. This drifts away in the tide attracting the mullet shoals until the fish actually nose the bag. Then it is a matter of lowering down your bait and hoping a fish takes. Remember that mullet have soft mouths and you will need a dropnet. In muddy creeks and rivers, legering at long range is best. Use harbour or king rag and watch the rod tip for a quick bite. If there is little tide you can even use a swingtip to show the bites.

The best, but most shy, mullet are invariably caught from isolated rock marks. These fish need stalking with the lightest of float tackle before they will take a bait. Pre-groundbaiting with minced mackerel and bread will bring the fish into the rock gullies where you stand a chance of catching them.

Location

Mullet cannot keep away from man. The dirtiest harbour, creek or dockside usually has its resident shoal of mullet in the summer. Any place where food scraps find their way into the water—such as under a pier—attracts mullet in their hundreds. They have a distinct preference for shallow, brackish water and will swim well up rivers into freshwater, where they are able to live quite happily. They spend much of their time lying motionless near the surface, or just basking in the sun. As the mullet grow larger, they seem to become more shy, frequenting rocks or the end of groynes. Some of the biggest mullet of all are taken from remote rock marks in the southwest, deep-water ports such as Dover or Portland, or desolate river mouths in Wales. Harbour or estuary mullet tend to run smaller. Mullet can be caught all round our shores, but they are at their most prolific along the south coast.

Harbours such as Christchurch and Portsmouth come alive during the summer with mullet grubbing around in the muddy shallows. Pier anglers from Southend round to Torquay seek them for their grand sport. Two sub-species, the thin-lipped and the golden-grey mullet, are found with the more common thick-lipped mullet. The former is recognised by its thinner top lip and smaller dorsal fins which are wider apart. The golden grey has a distinct golden blotch on the gill covers, and another smaller one behind the eye. Our picture is of the commoner thick-lipped mullet.

When to fish

Like most shy fish, early morning is the best time to take a mullet. Choose an incoming tide on a calm, still day and you will see the mullet shoals as they cut just beneath the surface. On a rough day, the mullet tend to stay deep although it is still possible to catch them. It is then that they are picked up by accident by the bottom angler after another fish. A fish of high summer, the mullet shoals tend to disperse at the start of the colder weather. Their breeding habits are still very much a mystery, although scientists tell us that they are a long-lived, slow-growing fish like the bass.

weed as it sucks them in. However, they can eat more solid food such as small worms and sand fly larvae.

The best natural bait for them is ragworm, preferably the small red harbour variety. Fish these in a bunch on the hook. Mullet will also take the bigger king rag, and occcasionally even maggots in fresh water. In Christchurch harbour—which probably holds the biggest mullet in the country—anglers fish for them with a small bar spoon, baited with a red ragworm, kept on the move. Old rotten lugworm can also work.

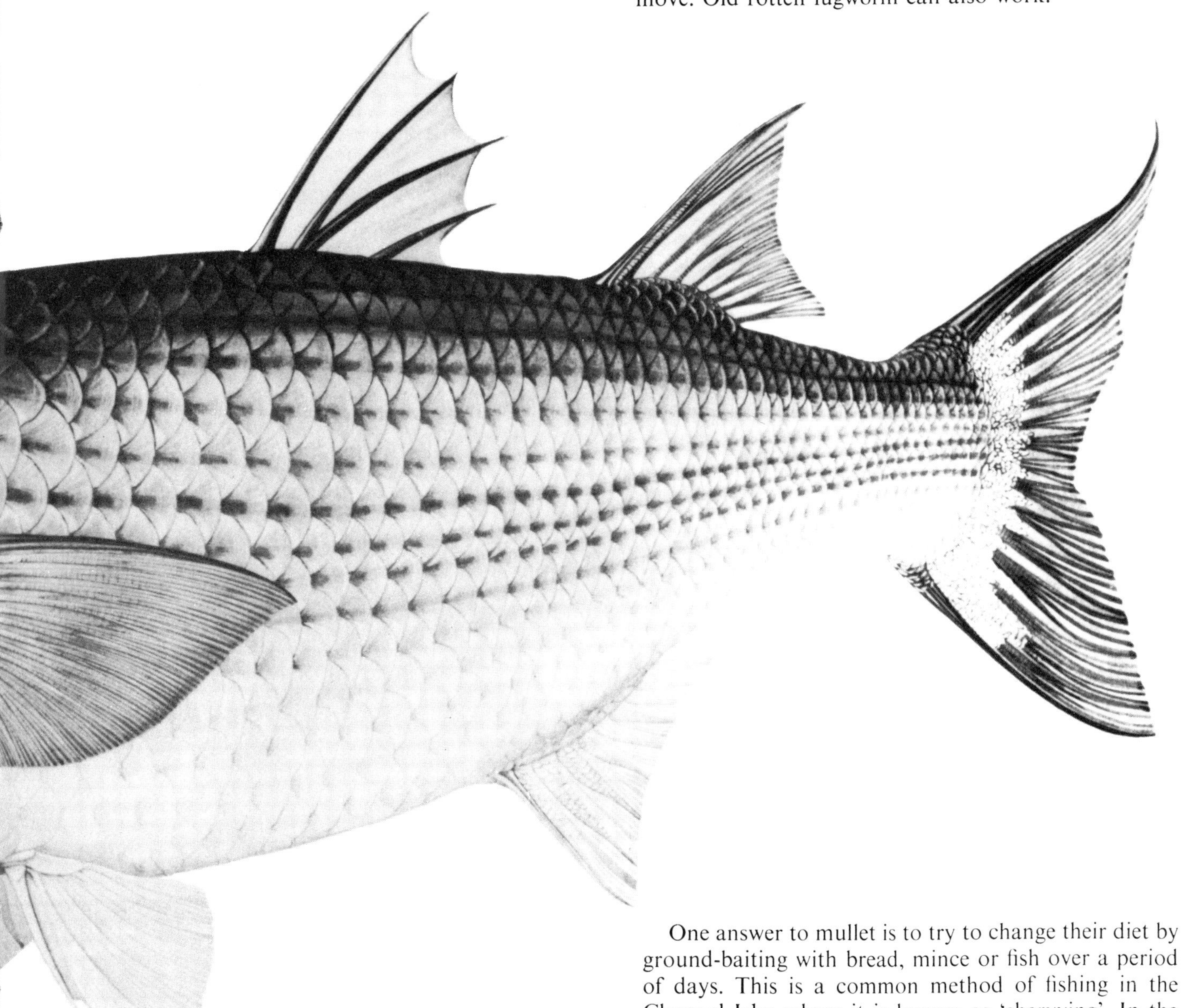

Baits

The mullet has a well-deserved reputation for being difficult to catch. Watch them browsing on the bottom mud and you will swear they will take your bait first cast. But nine times out of ten, the mullet will swim straight past!

The mullet's main diet is microscopic plant life, such as diatoms or algae, which it extracts from mud or

One answer to mullet is to try to change their diet by ground-baiting with bread, mince or fish over a period of days. This is a common method of fishing in the Channel Isles where it is known as 'shervying'. In the Southwest it is known as 'browsing.' There the locals use a mix made from pilchards. If you have ground-baited with fish, then try a small sliver of mackerel. Both baits can work well.

Mullet are naturally drawn to any food source, be it a sewer pipe or a canning factory. First you must experiment to find the right bait. Strange baits like bacon fat or herring roe have taken fish. At Leigh-on-Sea in the Thames estuary, where the cockles are cooked and sent to London, the favourite bait is cockles.

Index

Antenna float 20, 22-23, 29, 38
Arlesey bomb 34-35, 38, 42
Bacon fat 87
Balsa float 20, 22, 24-25, 26-27
Bananas 14
Barbel 6, 16, 30
Basket 8
Bass 59, 64-65, 67, 71, 80-81
Beach fishing 63-66
Beach tackle 50
Bite indicator 30-33, 38
Boat fishing 51-52, 67
Brandlings 16, 41
Breakaway grip lead 63
Bream 15, 16, 39, 47, 85
Bread 8, 16, 26, 39, 41, 42, 87
Butt indicator 33
Cane 22, 24, 30
Casters 15, 18-19, 21, 39, 41, 42, 43
Casting 6, 9, 53-57, 63, 65-66
Centre pin reel 6, 30, 52, 71, 78
Charter boat fishing 68
Cheese 16, 38, 42, 43
Chub 6, 15, 16, 21, 30, 42, 47
Clement's boom 78
Coalfish 70
Cockles 59, 83, 87
Cod 64, 67, 70, 71, 72, 74, 78-79
Conger 64, 66, 70, 71
Cork 22
Cove knot 36
Crab 59, 66, 78, 79, 80, 83
Dabs 64, 85
Dace 15, 46, 47
Dinghy fishing 67
Disgorger 8
Double grinner knot 37
Dough bobbin 30
Drilled bullet 34
Dropnet 51, 75
Ducker *see* Antenna float
Fibreglass 6, 31, 40
Fishbait 59, 66, 72, 85, 87
Fixed spool reel 6, 30, 50, 53, 71
Flatfish 59, 67, 72, 82-83
Float rod 6
Floats 7, 9, 20-29, 40, 44, 45, 46
Flounder 64
Fly fishing 44-45
Gaff 51, 66, 68
Garfish 71
Gozzers 15, 41
Grasshoppers 43
Grubb 44, 45
Gudgeon 45, 47
Halibut 82
Hemp 16, 39
Herring 47, 59, 79, 80, 85
Hooks 7, 44, 46, 51, 52
Indian reed *see* Sarkandas reed
Indicator *see* Bite indicator; Butt indicator
Jardine snap tackle 46
Keepnet 7
Knots 36-37
Landing net 7, 68
Leads 34-35
Legering 28, 30-35, 38, 42, 44, 45, 64-65, 67, 71, 80
Line 6-7, 30, 51, 52
  loading, 9
  sinking, 11
Ling 70
Live bait 46, 47
Lobworm 16, 38, 43, 44, 45
Lugworm 58, 59, 61-62, 54, 66, 72, 74, 78, 79, 82, 83, 87
Luncheon meat 16, 26
Mackerel 47, 59, 60, 68, 70, 71, 80, 83, 84, 85, 87
Maggots 8, 14, 39, 41, 42, 43, 44, 45, 47, 87
  see also Casters
    Gozzers
    Pinkies
    Squats
Mince 87
Minnows 44, 45
Missile *see* Antenna float
Mullet 51, 64, 67, 71, 86-87
Multiplier reel 50, 52, 53, 56-57, 78
Mussels 59, 79, 83
Nets 7
Nylon line 6, 46
Orange peel 14
Overhead cast 10-11
Paternoster link 35, 44, 45, 66, 72, 78, 86
Peacock quill float 20-21
Perch 16, 44-45
Pier fishing 71-75
Pike 46
Pilchards 59, 87
Pinkie 15-16, 38
Pirk 78
Pith 22
Plaice 64, 82-83
Pollack 70
Porcupine quill float 20
Pouting 71, 81
Quill float 20, 22, 38
Quiver tipping 30-32, 40
Ragworm 58, 72, 79, 80, 82, 83, 87
Redworms 16, 41
Reels 6, 50-51, 52
Roach 15, 16, 22, 38-39, 45, 46, 47
Rod rest 8, 30, 51
Rods 6, 50, 52
Rotten bottoms 78
Rudd 45
Salmon 42, 47
Sardine 47
Sarkandas reed 22, 38, 40
Sea baits 58-62
Seed baits 16-17
Shellfish 59, 72
Shock leader 63
Shot 7
Side casting reel 53, 54-55
Silicone rubber 30
Silver paper 14
Slider float 28-29, 44, 72, 76, 80
Slug 43, 45
Snail 43
Spade-end hooks 7
Sprat 47, 59, 78, 79, 81
Squat 15
Squid 59, 74, 79, 81, 83
Stick float 20-21, 24-25, 38
Stillwater fishing 33
Stone loach 45
Stop knot 28
Swan shot 7, 34, 42
Swimfeeders 35
Swinger *see* Antenna float
Swingtip cast 12-13, 30, 40
Tench 6, 16
Terry clip 33
Thornbacks 64, 66
Tip action rod 6
Tope 84-85
Treble hook 46
Trout 42, 47
Underarm cast 25
Valve rubber 30, 33
Waggler 21, 38
Wasp grub 26
Whiting 64, 67, 71, 72, 78, 79, 85
Worms 16, 26, 39, 41, 43, 44, 45, 47, 81
  see also Brandling
    Lobworm
    Lugworm
    Ragworm
    Redworm
Wrasse 64
Wreck fishing 67, 68
Zoomer *see* Antenna float

The Plaice